Deaf in America

Deaf in America

Voices from a Culture

Carol Padden

Tom Humphries

HARVARD UNIVERSITY PRESS
Cambridge, Massachusetts
London, England

Library of Congress Cataloging-in-Publication Data

Padden, Carol.
Deaf in America : voices from a culture /
. Carol Padden, Tom Humphries.
p.   cm.
Bibliography: p.
Includes index.
ISBN 0-674-19423-3 (alk. paper)
1. Deaf—United States.   I. Humphries, Tom.   II. Title.
HV2545.P33 1988   88-11769
362.4'2'0973—dc19   CIP

Preface

Our goal in planning this book was to collect, organize, and interpret examples of the cultural life of Deaf people. We came up with a range of very different materials, from childhood reminiscences of our friends to early films of signed performances to jokes and new forms of poetry in American Sign Language. The collection was broad and complex; instead of including everything we found, we have been selective. We admit to a preference for materials that are unusual or unexpected, that run counter to the more familiar ways of talking about Deaf people. We have organized these materials in a way that not only challenges the traditional orientation of describing Deaf people but also, we hope, contributes to ideas about human culture.

In order to stay close to Deaf people's lives and their stories, we have chosen not to write in detail about some topics that, while important and useful, would force us to assume a different style of writing. One example is the body of research on signed languages, especially American Sign Language (ASL). Rather than a chapter reviewing this research, we have written two chapters about how it has influenced the way Deaf people think and talk about their language.

Many of our best sources of information are ones that have been overlooked in the past as "amateur" or "casual," largely because they are not written but signed. But as we plan to show, they are as vital and essential to the description of Deaf people as more "formal" material. Some of them are recorded on film or videotape, but we also describe public performances that have not been recorded. In these cases we use reports of viewers or participants.

We have adopted some guidelines for the protection of the people whose comments, stories, or anecdotes appear here. If the material we discuss has been published or, to our knowledge, is publicly available, as in the case of some videotaped materials, we use the real names of the people involved. We also use the real names of participants in public performances. Otherwise, in the case of anecdotes and informally told stories, the names we give are fictitious.

In our search for new stores of information, we were greatly helped by colleagues who provided or alerted us to stories, home movies, performances, and written work by Deaf people. We would like especially to acknowledge the assistance of Linda Bove, Byron B. Burnes, Mel Carter, James De Bee, J. B. Davis, Bea Davis, Bernard Bragg, Patricia De Caro, Larry Fleischer, Jack Gannon, Patrick Graybill, Corrine Hilton, Ella Lentz, Eric Malzkuhn, Dorothy Miles, Grace Mudgett, Freda Norman, Agnes Padden, Donald Padden, Carlene Pederson, Ruth Phillips, John Schuchman, Cheri Smith, Ted Supalla, Sam Supalla, Clayton Valli, Ed Waterstreet, and others whose stories helped us to make the critical connections but who remain anonymous. Funds from the Laurent Clerc Cultural Fund, administered by the Gallaudet University Alumni Association, were instrumental in helping us to locate new and overlooked material as well as in allowing us time away from other commitments to complete the book.

We are also grateful to Michael Cole and Margaret Griffin for their key insights into the relationship between culture and history, and to Emmett Casey, Harlan Lane, David Laitin, David Perlmutter, Frank Philip, Michael Schudson, James Wertsch, and our anonymous reviewers, who, with great persuasion and sensitivity, pushed us to recognize deeper issues in our work. We thank Lisa Hirschman for a suggestion that helped shape Chapter 6. We also acknowledge the highly capable and thorough assistance of our editors, Michael Aronson and Camille Smith, at Harvard University Press.

The technical aspects of the book could not have been better supported than by our illustrators: Robert Hills, Peggy Swartzel-Lott, and Daniel Renner. Ella Lentz and Freda Norman graciously agreed to recreate poetry and performances for our illustrations. Merrie Davidson provided valuable assistance on other aspects of manuscript preparation, including the compilation of the index.

Contents

Introduction

The traditional way of writing about Deaf people is to focus on the fact of their condition—that they do not hear—and to interpret all other aspects of their lives as consequences of this fact. Our goal in this book is to write about Deaf people in a new and different way. In contrast to the long history of writings that treat them as medical cases, or as people with "disabilities," who "compensate" for their deafness by using sign language, we want to portray the lives they live, their art and performances, their everyday talk, their shared myths, and the lessons they teach one another. We have always felt that the attention given to the physical condition of not hearing has obscured far more interesting facets of Deaf people's lives.

Our exploration is partly a personal one: the lives of Deaf people include our own. Carol was born deaf in a Deaf family. Her parents and her older brother are Deaf, as are a set of grandparents and some other relatives. Tom, in contrast, became deaf as a child and did not meet other Deaf people until he entered a college for Deaf students.

Our professional interests over the last ten years have also led us to this topic. We have both participated in a new generation of research on signed language. Carol has written technical descriptions of the structure of American Sign Language, and Tom has written about approaches to teaching English to Deaf people that recognize signed language as a central instrument. With our colleagues, we have uncovered significant details about signed languages that had never been thought about before, let alone described. The sum of this research is that signed languages are far from the primitive gestural systems they had been assumed to be. Instead they are rich systems with complex structures that reflect their long histories. Thinking about the linguistic richness uncovered in our work has made us realize that the language has developed through the generations as part of an equally rich cultural heritage. It is this heritage—the culture of Deaf people—that we want to begin to portray in this book.

———— • ————

Before beginning our journey through the imagery and patterns of meaning that constitute Deaf people's lives, we must identify the community of "Deaf" people with which we are concerned. Following a convention proposed by James Woodward (1972), we use the lowercase *deaf* when referring to the audiological condition of not hearing, and the uppercase *Deaf* when referring to a particular group of deaf people who share a language— American Sign Language (ASL)—and a culture. The members of this group reside in the United States and Canada, have inherited their sign language, use it as a primary means of communication among themselves, and hold a set of beliefs about themselves and their connection to the larger society. We distinguish them from, for example, those who find themselves losing their hearing because of illness, trauma or age; although these people share the condition of not hearing, they do not have access to the knowledge, beliefs, and practices that make up the culture of Deaf people. As we will emphasize in subsequent chapters, this knowledge of Deaf people is not simply a camaraderie with others who have a similar physical condition, but is, like many other cultures in the traditional sense of the term, historically created and actively transmitted across generations.

Woodward's distinction, while useful, is not an entirely clear-cut one. For example, consider deaf children from hearing families who encounter Deaf people and their culture outside the family. At what point are they said to have adopted the conventions of the culture and become Deaf? This question also applies to the acculturation processes of deaf adults who, after spending many years apart from Deaf people, come to join the community at later ages. Markowicz and Woodward (1978) have suggested that self-identification with the group and skill in ASL should be important diagnostic factors in deciding who is Deaf. But the bounded distinction between the terms *Deaf* and *deaf* represents only part of the dynamic of how Deaf people talk about themselves. Deaf people are both Deaf and deaf, and their discussions, even arguments, over issues of identity show that these two categories are often interrelated in complex ways. We explore these complexities in more detail in Chapter 3, including the cases of two groups who pose special problems for the culture: newly arrived deaf persons who have yet to learn the full range of skills required for the culture, and hearing children from Deaf families. A newly arrived deaf person is often given one of several borderline labels, such as "hard of hearing," recognizing his or her past affiliation with those who speak. Hearing children of Deaf parents represent an ongoing contradiction in the culture: they display the knowledge of their parents—skill in the language and social conduct—but the culture finds subtle ways to give them an unusual and separate status.

Also following Woodward, we use the term *Deaf* in this book to refer to other cultures of people who do not hear and who use sign languages other than ASL. In Quebec, for example, Deaf French Canadians use a different sign language, Langue des Signes Québecois. Nova Scotia has a community of Deaf people whose sign language is related to British Sign Language but not to ASL. In fact, in nearly every nation in the world there are several distinct groups of Deaf people, their differences marked by political, historical, or geographical separation.

Although we recognize that there are many cultures of Deaf people, without detailed ethnographies of various groups we cannot offer generalizations about them or about the relationship between the condition of not hearing and the formation of a culture. This book is about the Deaf culture we know best, our own.

Even within the population of Deaf people who use ASL, not surprisingly, there is enormous diversity. Large communities of Deaf people in Boston, Chicago, Los Angeles, and Edmonton, Alberta, to give a few examples, have their own distinctive identities. Within these local communities there are smaller groups organized by class, profession, ethnicity, or race, each of which has yet another set of distinct characteristics. Until about 1970, racial segregation in the larger society dictated that white and black deaf children in the southern states should attend separate schools. Although teachers in black deaf schools knew the white variety of ASL, the segregation led to the development of a distinct black variety, which is still used by black Deaf adults in certain regions of the South, although many also know the white variety (Woodward 1976; Maxwell and Smith-Todd 1986). Cities like Washington, D.C., and New York have large black Deaf clubs that are active centers for their communities. But all these subgroups of the category of Deaf people have in common the use of some variety of ASL.

There are no reliable figures on the number of Deaf people in the United States and Canada. Health statistics lead to an estimate of the occurrence of "hearing impairment" in the general population at 9 percent (U.S. National Center for Health Statistics 1987). But teasing out the smaller number of Deaf people from such estimates is difficult at best.

One reason for this difficulty is that, as we have said, the fact of not hearing is not itself a determinant of group identity. Although the term "deaf" is the group's official label for itself, people who are Deaf can have a range of hearing abilities from "hard of hearing" to "profoundly deaf," and, conversely, there are people with severe or profound hearing impairment who do not participate in the community of Deaf people. Another reason is that there are no figures on the number of users of signed language in the United States and Canada. Based on estimates of numbers of people who attended schools where they were extensively exposed to Deaf people and signed language, and on the number of Deaf people known to social service agencies, there are estimates of the Deaf population in the neighborhood of a few hundred thousand.

The unique pattern of cultural transmission within the group compounds the problem of estimating its numbers. Although somewhere between 11 and 30 percent of deaf schoolchildren inherit their deafness, fewer than 10 percent are born to parents who are also Deaf. Consequently, in contrast to the situation in most cultures, the great majority of individuals within the community of Deaf people do not join it at birth.

———•———

This unique pattern of transmission lies at the heart of the culture. As will be seen in some of the stories in later chapters, one of its consequences is the central role the school plays in the community. Many of these stories refer to "residential schools," the type of schools most of today's Deaf adults attended. These are boarding schools, usually state-funded, specifically for deaf children from as young as preschool through high school. Almost every state and province in the United States and Canada funded at least one "school for the deaf" between 1817, the year the first public school for deaf children was founded, and 1980 (Schildroth 1980; Gannon 1981). Children attending these boarding schools typically return home only for weekends and holidays. Many older Deaf people spent large portions of their early lives at these schools, going home only at Christmas or during summers.

Although there are some "oral" residential schools, which officially disallow the use of signed language, most residential schools are "manual" schools, in which signed language is allowed in classrooms. Even in these schools, however, educational policy typically emphasizes speech and the English language; sign language and other practices of Deaf people are rarely given a central part in school policies. As some of the stories we have collected suggest, in subtle ways deaf children manage to circumvent the will of "obstructionist" adults to teach one another the knowledge of Deaf people.

In many of these schools, deaf children spend years of their lives among Deaf people—children from Deaf families and Deaf adults who work at the school. Many schools are staffed to some extent by Deaf people who graduated from the same school or another one like it. For these deaf children, the most significant aspect of residential life is the dormitory. In the dormitories, away from the structured control of the classroom, deaf children are introduced to the social life of Deaf people. In the informal dormitory environment children learn not only sign language but the content of the culture. In this way, the schools become hubs of the communities that surround them, preserving for the next generation the culture of earlier generations.

The residential school is not the only avenue for introduction to the community. Some deaf children do not leave home to attend residential schools but, like both of us, stay home and go to public school with "the others," as hearing people are called. Tom remained among his hearing neighbors and relatives, and in various ways adapted to the demands of his school. Only later, as an adult, did he meet other Deaf people. In Carol's case, her Deaf parents and older brother attended residential schools, but because she is "hard of hearing" she was judged to be more likely to withstand the demands of a "speaking environment" and went to public school instead. Each way of entering the community carries its own issues of identity and shared knowledge; we discuss these further in a later chapter.

————— • —————

As we have said, one of the primary identifying characteristics of the group is its language. The history of the education of deaf children in America is marked by almost total ignorance about the place of signed languages in the family of human languages, ignorance that has been translated in tragic ways into social and educational policy. But despite these pressures, American Sign

Language has had a durable history. Its origins can be traced to the emergence of a large community of deaf people centered around the first public school for deaf children in France, founded about 1761; the language that arose in this community is still being used in France today. In 1817, a Deaf teacher from this school helped establish the first public school for deaf children in the United States. Although his language was incorporated into the early curriculum, the children's own gestural systems mingled with the official signed language, resulting in a new form that was no longer identifiable as French Sign Language. Some signs and structures in ASL today still reflect their French Sign Language origins, although the two languages are distinct.

According to the common misconceptions about ASL, it is either a collection of individual gestures or a code on the hands for spoken English. But in fact, although ASL does use gesture, as English uses sound, it is not made up merely of gestures any more than English is made up merely of noises. Individual signs are themselves structured grammatical units, which are placed in slots within sentences according to grammatical rules. Signs are not a form of "fingerspelling," a manual system in which a hand configuration is used to represent a letter of the alphabet. Although signers may fingerspell an English term or a name, the bulk of their signed communication is made up not of fingerspelling but of signs, which are structured according to an entirely independent set of rules.

To give just one example, ASL verbs can be divided into three major classes (Padden 1988b). Verbs in one class can inflect for person and number of both the subject and the object; these include GIVE, SEND, TAKE, CATCH.[1] Those in another class do not inflect for person and number at all; they include LEARN,

---

1. Signs are represented by English translations in small capital letters. If more than one English word is needed to translate a sign, the words are joined by hyphens. Small capital letters joined by hyphens represent fingerspelled words or abbreviations. These translations, of course, can only be approximate, and often do not express the full range of meaning of the sign.

LIKE, VISIT, TELEPHONE. Verbs in the third class also cannot inflect for person and number, but can take an extremely rich range of affixes.[2]

These verb forms, which demonstrate that ASL is far more complex than a mere system of gestures, also form one small part of a large body of evidence that it is not based on English. The set of rules for word formation—that is, the morphology—of ASL verbs does not resemble that of English verbs. English verbs inflect only for person and number of the *subject*. Not all ASL verbs inflect for person and number, as we have said, but the ones that do largely inflect for person and number of the subject *and the object*. Compared to other spoken languages, English has comparatively impoverished verb morphology; in contrast, some ASL verbs are as rich as those in spoken languages with complex verb morphology, such as Navajo and Southern Tiwa (Padden 1988b; Supalla 1985; Klima et al. 1979).

Another piece of evidence that ASL is independent of English can be found in its sentence structure. For example, in English it is correct to say either "I gave the book to him" or "I gave him the book." But in ASL only the second structure, called the dative, is possible. The signed sequence I-GIVE-HIM MAN BOOK ("I gave a man a book") is correct, but I-GIVE-HIM BOOK MAN is ungrammatical (Padden 1988b). In this particular way ASL resembles not English but languages unrelated to English, such as the Mayan language, Tzotzil (Aissen 1983), which permit only dative structures.

Evidence like this is used by linguists to demonstrate that although signed languages and spoken languages differ in their forms, they do not differ in their sets of possible structures. ASL

---

2. For short reviews of signed language structure see Padden (1986, 1988a), Wilbur (1986), and Siple (1982); for more extensive reviews see texts by Wilbur (1979, 1987), Kyle and Woll (1983), Lane and Grosjean (1980), Bellugi and Studdert-Kennedy (1980), Baker (1980), Baker and Battison (1980), Klima et al. (1979), and Siple (1978). These sources provide more extensive arguments supporting structures proposed for specific signed languages.

is unlike English in sentence structure, but its structures resemble those of other natural languages.

The mistaken belief that ASL is a set of simple gestures with no internal structure has led to the tragic misconception that the relationship of Deaf people to their sign language is a casual one that can be easily severed and replaced. This misconception more than any other has driven educational policy. Generations of schoolchildren have been forbidden to use signs and compelled to speak. Other children have been urged to use artifically modified signs in place of vocabulary from their natural sign language.

This misconception has also found its way into the culture, as can be seen in the ways Deaf people talk about their language. Even though they talk of ASL as something highly valued, almost in the same breath they may reason that if ASL does not qualify as a language, it follows that, for their own good, deaf children should give it up in favor of a "real" language, specifically a spoken one, or at least a form of signing "based" on a spoken language. Despite the misconceptions, for Deaf people, their sign language is a creation of their history and is what allows them to fulfill the potential for which evolution has prepared them—to attain full human communication as makers and users of symbols.

———•———

A large population, established patterns of cultural transmission, and a common language: these are all basic ingredients for a rich and inventive culture. Yet in looking at written descriptions of Deaf people, we could find little about their cultural life. We could remember being profoundly moved by signed performances, but we found little analysis of the kinds of performances we had seen. We would listen to anecdotes told by our friends and feel a powerful resonance with our own lives, but we rarely saw anything about these experiences or these feelings in print.

As many before us have observed, most descriptive materials about Deaf people's lives center around the condition of not hearing. In a summary of papers on the subject written between 1975 and 1982, James Woodward (1982) documents the existence of a widespread and powerful interpretation of Deaf people as "pathological" and "fundamentally deficient." This ideology has led students of the Deaf community to describe in detail the facts of hearing impairment, and to classify Deaf people in terms of the degree of their impairment. Other facts about them, notably those about their social and cultural lives, are then interpreted as consequences of these classifications.

A classic example of this approach can be found in a survey of "hearing impaired school leavers," or graduates from British schools for deaf children. Rodda (1970) categorized each hearing-impaired leaver according to hearing type, then correlated hearing type with a long list of social characteristics such as having a savings account, pursuing certain hobbies, attending church, and having friends who were "similarly afflicted." The last description in particular makes clear the focus on the pathological: hearing children who choose hearing playmates are not described as preferring "similarly afflicted" friends. The thrust of Rodda's research is that a physical condition, rather than other determining factors such as socioeconomic class or group affiliation, underlies all choices Deaf people make in their lives.

In introductory texts on educating deaf children, to give another example, the first few chapters are obligatorily devoted to hearing loss, and then the fact of this loss is incorporated into discussions of the task of education. As Erting (1985a, 1985b) and others have pointed out, the focus in deaf education is on the audiological. For the writers of such textbooks, the most compelling fact about deaf children is their inability to hear, which in turn requires that they receive special training in speaking and hearing. In contrast, the textbooks rarely explore ways to introduce the resources of Deaf culture to young deaf children who have not been exposed to it.

In our work, we adopt an approach that begins not with hearing loss but with the cultural world. Using theories from the study of human cultures, we focus not on a direct relationship between people's physical features and their behavior but on an examination of the place of these features and behavior in their larger cultural life. In a variety of ways, Deaf people have accumulated a set of knowledge about themselves in the face of the larger society's understanding—or misunderstanding—of them. They have found ways to define and express themselves through their rituals, tales, performances, and everyday social encounters. The richness of their sign language affords them the possibilities of insight, invention, and irony. In exploring this culture, we have collected an array of materials that suggest a new way to order information about what it means to be Deaf. Using these materials, we have tried to present the culture from the inside— to discover how Deaf people describe themselves, what sorts of symbols they surround themselves with, and how they think about their lives.

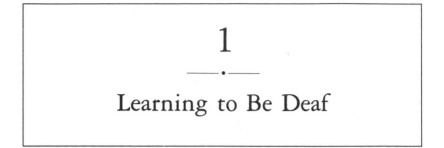

1

Learning to Be Deaf

When we began work on this book, we had collected a store of reminiscences from Deaf adults about their childhoods; many told how as young children they discovered that they could not hear sound or speech. For example, in a story that appears in a videotaped version of a stage production by the National Theatre of the Deaf, Dorothy Miles recalls how, after a long childhood illness, she discovers that she can no longer hear her own voice. These are the expected anecdotes, those which confirm the popular wisdom about deafness—that it is the experience of not hearing. But we also came across stories that, although they were about discovering deafness, seemed only remotely connected to the fact of loss of hearing. One such example came from an interview Carol conducted with two sisters, one five and the other seven years old, as part of a study on language learning in the home. Both girls are Deaf, as are their parents. After an afternoon of tests and conversation, the younger girl, Vicki, brought a toy for Carol to inspect:

Vicki: My friend Michael gave it to me.
Helen: Michael's her boyfriend. (giggles)
Vicki: Michael is not! Anyway Michael is Deaf.
Helen: No! Michael is hearing!
Vicki: (confused, but not convinced) Michael is Deaf!
Helen: You're wrong! I know! Michael is hearing.
Carol: Well, which is he? Deaf or hearing?

Vicki: (pauses) I don't know.
Carol: What do you think?
Vicki: Both! Michael is Deaf and hearing!

The solution was immensely satisfying to Vicki, but her older sister was aghast. No one is ever both Deaf and hearing at the same time. One is either Deaf or hearing. But Vicki had become attached to her explanation. After repeatedly telling Vicki that her solution would not work, Helen threw up her hands in exasperation and complained to their parents. The adults, of course, found the girls' argument yet another amusing example of the marvelously inventive logic of children.

Let us look closer at the conversation. Vicki believes that her friend Michael is Deaf. And she evidently considers this fact a notable one, since she mentions it when she presents her toy to Carol. She has learned that, in the world of her parents and their friends, when one wishes to say something of note about someone, terms like "Deaf" and "hearing" are obligatory. Even at age five, she knows that in conversations about people one needs to refer to the person's status. This conversation would have continued unremarkably except for the fact that Vicki was wrong about Michael.

What apparently has impressed Vicki about Michael is that he uses signs. To her, hearing people do not use signed language and therefore lack ways to make themselves understood. To her, Michael's ability to converse with her in her language is sufficient evidence that he is Deaf. But the older child knows better: there are characteristics other than signing that determine whether someone is really Deaf.

Children are astute observers of the world—they are often "wrong" for the most interesting reasons and "right" for reasons we never expect. This quality makes them revealing theorists. As we see in Vicki's case, a child's insight can be useful for bringing out hidden definitions for a supposedly straightforward word like "deaf."

When Vicki reaches her older sister's age, she will be able to identify other elusive but important properties from which one can deduce whether a person is Deaf. At age seven, Helen can detect subtle differences in movement contours between native or very fluent signers and those who have learned the language relatively recently; she knows that inexperienced signers often distort circular movements or add wrong movements to signs. She also watches how the person mouths while signing; skilled signers mouth along with signs in characteristic ways, and unskilled signers mouth in yet another recognizable style. And she is better able than Vicki to decipher the meanings of signs; a wrong choice of sign in a sentence might tip her off to the signer's true status. Hearing children of Deaf parents sometimes confuse her if they sign as well as their parents, but this is a mistake even her own parents might make. And Helen has also learned that another of Michael's characteristics is his ability to hear.

One might expect that characteristics other than signing would be important in distinguishing Deaf from hearing persons: the ability or the inability to speak, or even the ability or inability to hear sound. But these seem irrelevant to Vicki. There may be an easy explanation for this: Deaf children cannot hear, thus perhaps they do not appreciate the ability of others to perceive sound.

We think this explanation is too simple. We do not believe that Vicki's conception of the world simply lacks an "auditory" sense and that her view of the world is consequently limited to what remains. Instead, we believe her "error" is typical of young children her age who are forming hypotheses about how the world works. Vicki's error is an attempt to formulate an analysis of the world within the set of assumptions and ideas to which she has been exposed. The assumptions and ideas in this case involve her family's ways of determining the status of visitors, such as whether Michael is Deaf or hearing. A hearing child would have an equally restricted range of possible guesses about the world, based on the beliefs shared by the family. For example, white middle-class children understand that black people have some distinctive physical characteristic, but they are sometimes confused about who is to be called "black"; we know one young child who refers to all dark-haired men as black.

———— • ————

Sam Supalla once described to us his childhood friendship with a hearing girl who lived next door (this account also appears in Perlmutter 1986). As Sam's story went, he had never lacked for playmates; he was born into a Deaf family with several Deaf older brothers. As his interests turned to the world outside his family, he noticed a girl next door who seemed to be about his age. After a few tentative encounters, they became friends. She was a satisfactory playmate, but there was the problem of her "strangeness." He could not talk with her as he could with his older brothers and his parents. She seemed to have extreme difficulty understanding even the simplest or crudest gestures. After a few futile attempts to converse, he gave up and instead pointed when he wanted something, or simply dragged her along with him if he wanted to go somewhere. He wondered what strange affliction his friend had, but since they had developed a way to interact with each other, he was content to accommodate to her peculiar needs.

One day, Sam remembers vividly, he finally understood that his friend was indeed odd. They were playing in her home, when suddenly her mother walked up to them and animatedly began to move her mouth. As if by magic, the girl picked up a dollhouse and moved it to another place. Sam was mystified and went home to ask his mother about exactly what kind of affliction the girl next door had. His mother explained that she was HEARING and because of this did not know how to SIGN; instead she and her mother TALK, they move their mouths to communicate with each other. Sam then asked if this girl and her family were the only ones "like that." His mother explained that no, in fact, nearly everyone else was like the neighbors. It was his own family that was unusual. It was a memorable moment for Sam. He remembers thinking how curious the girl next door was, and if she was HEARING, how curious HEARING people were.

When Sam discovers that the girl next door is hearing, he learns something about "others." Those who live around him and his family are now to be called "hearing." The world is larger than he previously thought, but his view of himself is intact. He has learned that there are "others" living in his neighborhood, but he has not yet learned that others have different ways of thinking. Perhaps others are now more prominent in his world, and his thoughts about the world now have to acknowledge that they exist in some relation to himself, but it does not occur to him that these others might define him and his family by some characteristic they lack.

In fact, in almost all the stories of childhood we have heard from Deaf children of Deaf families, hearing people were "curious" and "strange" but mostly were part of the background. The children's world was large enough with family and friends that the existence of "others" was not disruptive. At the age when children begin to reflect on the world, we see an interesting positioning of the self with respect to "others," people like Sam's playmate and her mother. Sam has not yet understood that the outside world considers him and his family to have an "affliction"; to him, immersed in the world of his family, it is the neighbors who lack the ability to communicate.

————•————

But before long, the world of others inevitably intrudes. We can see children learning about the minds of others in stories Deaf adults tell about their childhoods. A Deaf friend of ours, Howard, a prominent member of his community, made a revealing comment to a mixed audience of hearing and Deaf people. All members of his family—his parents and brother as well as aunts and uncles—are Deaf. He told the audience that he had spent his early childhood among Deaf people but that when he was six his world changed: his parents took him to a school for Deaf children. "Would you believe," he said, pausing expertly for effect, "I never knew I was deaf until I first entered school?"

Howard's comment caused the intended stir in the audience, but it was clear to us that some people thought it meant that Howard first became aware of his audiological deficiency when he was six—that he had never realized before that he could not hear sounds. But this was not his meaning at all.

Howard certainly knew what "deaf" meant. The sign DEAF was part of his everyday vocabulary; he would refer to DEAF people whenever he needed to talk about family and friends, in much the same way as Vicki mentioned that Michael was DEAF. When Howard arrived at school, he found that teachers used the same sign he used for himself at home, DEAF. But it did not take him long to detect a subtle difference in the ways they used the sign.

The child uses DEAF to mean "us," but he meets others for whom "deaf" means "them, not like us." He thinks DEAF means "friends who behave as expected," but to others it means "a remarkable condition." At home he has taken signing for granted as an activity hardly worth noticing, but he will learn at school that it is something to be talked about and commented on. Depending on what school a child attends, he may be forbidden to use signed language in the presence of his teachers. He will then have to learn how to carry out familiar activities within new boundaries, to learn new social contexts for his language. Skills he learned at home, such as to tell stories with detail about people and events, are not likely to be rewarded by teachers who do not know the language. His language will be subordinated to other activities considered more important, notably learning how to "use his hearing," and to "speak" (Erting 1985b).

The metaphor of affliction, as it is used to describe deaf children, represents a displacement from the expected, that is, from the hearing child. Howard and Sam were used to a certain mode of exchange at home, certain ways in which Deaf friends and family acknowledge each other. But the alien organization of the school, from its hierarchical structure and its employment of hearing people to its insistence on speech, makes plain to the child that an entirely different set of assumptions is in force. Even the familiar—adults in his school whom he recognizes as DEAF—do not and cannot behave in the same ways they do in his community; their roles must change in the face of the demands of an institution that largely belongs to others (Erting 1985a).

The child "discovers" deafness. Now deafness becomes a prominent fact in his life, a term around which people's behavior changes. People around him have debates about deafness, and lines are sharply drawn between people depending on what position they take on the subject. He has never thought about himself as having a certain quality, but now it becomes something to discuss. Even his language has ceased to be just a means of interacting with others and has become an object: people are either "against" signed language or "for" signed language. In the stories we have collected from Deaf children of Deaf parents, the same pattern emerges over and over: "deafness" is "discovered" late and in the context of these layers of meaning.

It is not surprising that the school is often the setting for this kind of discovery. School is not the only place where Deaf children meet others, of course, but the realization that others have different ways of thinking, and that these ways of thinking are influential in the school, is forced upon them when they arrive.

Bernard Bragg, in a personal story about his Deaf mother, represents in spatial terms the vast distance between the home and the world of others. We have translated this story from a videotaped record of the National Theatre of the Deaf's original production *My Third Eye* (1973):

> I asked again where we were going but she gave no reply. For the first time I began to feel a sense of fear and foreboding. I stole glances at her face, but it was immobile and her eyes were fixed on an unseen place somewhere ahead. We rode for a long time, and then we stopped and found ourselves in front of an enormous building . . . We walked into the building, and once inside I was immediately struck by a

medicinal, institutional smell. This did not look like a hospital, or like any other building I had seen before. My mother bent down, turned me toward her, and said: "This is where you will get all your education. You will live here for a while. Don't worry, I will see you again later." Then she couldn't seem to say any more, she hugged me quickly, gave me a kiss, and then, inexplicably, left.[1]

The spotlight dims and Bragg disappears in the darkness. The audience feels a brief but powerful sense of loss. For generations of Deaf people who have left home for school, this story evokes intense images of encountering more than just an unknown place. Bragg chooses powerful triggers: his mother's unusual inarticulateness, the looming size of the school building, the cavernous halls, and the sharpest image of all, the unfamiliar, faintly threatening institutional smell. The smell wraps around him, frightening him, and when he reaches for his mother she is gone. Her parting words, about education and school, are hardly comforting.

———— • ————

We have been discussing Deaf children of Deaf families, but deaf children in hearing families face an equally unusual and complementary dilemma. Compare Howard's and Sam's stories with that of Tony, a child of a hearing family who learns that, as a result of medical treatment of childhood diseases, he has become deaf at age six.

I don't remember any one moment when I thought to myself, "I can't hear." Rather it was slowly assimilating a combination of different things. I had been ill for a long time. I remember the repeated visits to the doctor, until finally somehow I sensed a permanence to what had been happening to me. I remember my parents worrying about me, and at some point everyone seemed concerned about my

1. Translated by Carol Padden and Tom Humphries.

illness. It was at that point I felt changed, and when I thought about how I was changed, my thought was: "I'm the only one like this."

When this child referred to himself as "deaf," he meant an intensely individual and personal condition. The illness had affected him and no one else in his family. There were no others like himself:

I had a second cousin who was deaf but I decided I wasn't like her at all. She used her hands, she signed. I wasn't like her—I talked and I was like everyone else, except I couldn't hear. There wasn't anyone else in my hometown who was deaf, except I guess for this woman down the road we called "mute," who lived with her sister. She didn't talk and she and her sister had this private home sign language they used with each other. I wasn't any of them.

For Tony, being deaf meant being set apart from his family and friends; he was "deaf" and had had an "illness." In contrast, Sam, the Deaf child of Deaf parents, thought of being "Deaf" not as a consequence of some event, but simply as a given. For Sam, "Deaf" was not a term used to refer to him personally, but was just a normal way of describing himself and everyone he knew.

Another child of hearing parents, Jim, told us that his hearing loss was not diagnosed until he was almost seven years old (his "difficulties" were attributed to other causes). He remembered that as a child, "I thought everyone lipread. But it always puzzled me that others seemed to lipread better than I could." Later, when his loss was discovered, he began to wear a hearing aid, and his new teachers taught him another way of describing the difference between himself and others. He was told that the difference didn't have to do with lipreading ability; it had to do with his not being able to hear.

In contrast to Vicki and Helen, who watch people's signing abilities, Jim was attentive to mouthing behaviors of the people around him, who did not sign. As a very young child he was probably not aware that he was "lipreading," but he knew oral behaviors were important in social exchanges.

As an exercise contrasting Sam and Howard's world with that of Tony and Jim, let us imagine under what sorts of dependencies or conditions certain behaviors follow others in Deaf and hearing families. In Deaf families, people signal one another by touching or by making a movement into another's visual range. Making a small vibration on a table or the floor is also possible, and for some people in certain ranges, one can call loudly. After one person acknowledges the other, they begin to interact in other ways. They look at each other, and they use signs.

But in a hearing family, the types of behaviors used to signal one another are different. One person can move his mouth and cause another person's behavior to change. And they do not even have to be visible to each other; someone can move his mouth and make another person come into the room. Once one person acknowledges the other, they alternate moving mouths. Sometimes they look at each other, but sometimes they do not.

We can imagine that Jim, a deaf child whose hearing family did not even realize he was deaf, must have noticed "strange" dependencies between events and behaviors. One behavior would suddenly be provoked, and it would not be clear to the young boy what the stimulus was. Imagine Jim sitting in a room near a door. Suddenly his mother appears, walking purposefully to the door. She opens the door, and there is a visitor waiting on the doorstep. But if the child opens the door at another time, odds are that no visitor will be there. How does the child, who does not hear the doorbell, understand what the stimulus is for the odd behavior of opening a door and finding someone standing there? We can only guess. We know only that Jim assumed other people had powers not yet discernible to him, such as better lipreading skills.

———— • ————

Jim's story and the other stories we have recounted are about how children learn the significant arrangements of their worlds. Jim's theory about other people's lipreading powers is not a bad one; it is consistent with our point that his hypotheses follow from the set of assumptions held by his family about how to conduct one's life. What Jim's and the other cases have in common is that being able or unable to hear does not emerge as significant in itself; instead it takes on significance in the context of other sets of meaning to which the child has been exposed.

As a final example to drive home this point, we turn to the story of Joe, the youngest child of a Deaf family on a farm in the heart of Indiana. Joe told us, "I never knew I was hearing until I was six. I never suspected in any way that I was different from my parents and siblings."

It seems ludicrous to imagine a hearing child who does not know he can hear. Is a child like this unresponsive to sounds? Are we to imagine a hearing child who discovers sound at the age of six? Of course not. Joe did know about sound. He responded to sounds, and his conception of the world included sound. But in the flow of everyday life he had no cause to think about sound in anything but an incidental way. He probably thought about it as often and as consciously as children reflect on the fact that they have feet.

The key part of his comment lies in the sentence "I never suspected I was in any way different from my parents and siblings." This is not a case of pretended deafness; Joe did not fail to hear, but simply understood sound in a way he could reconcile with the experiences of his family. We can imagine a range of phenomena in this child's world that have double but compatible interpretations: a spoon falls and makes a sound as it hits the floor. Someone picks it up, not simply because it made a sound but because it slipped from view. The farmer goes out to milk the cows not only because they make noises, but because it is daybreak, the time set aside for milking. A door slams, air rushes into the room, and objects on the table rattle and wobble. Many sounds coincide with nonauditory events, to which Joe would have seen his parents responding. His parents' world gave him no reason to identify sound as a primary cause of events.

One might ask how a hearing child would understand a sound

that had no corresponding nonauditory event. What if the door slammed in another room and his family did not respond? Would he not see this as odd, or even as a contradiction? We might imagine a moment when the child is startled by a loud noise, looks at his family, and is puzzled by their lack of response. But the child does not yet have a basis for being "puzzled." He does not have an alternative explanation. The most striking observation hearing children of Deaf parents make about their early years is that it never occurs to them until they are older that there is anything unusual about their abilities. For young children immersed in the world of their families, there is not yet space for contradictions.

These stories by adults about their childhood memories reveal a rare perspective on the question of how the world comes to mean what it does. The conventional belief is that there are certain immutable events, such as sound, that do not need translation and can be known directly. But Joe's story reminds us that very little is not filtered through the larger pattern of everyday life. Sound is not an entity that is free of interpretation, but something that emerges within a system of knowledge. One does not merely "hear" thunder, but also must assimilate its place in relation to all other activity of the world, how to react to it, how to talk about it, how to know its relationship to other sounds. For both Deaf and hearing people, sound finds its place against the larger pattern of everyday life.

———— • ————

Up to this point we have been vague in our references to the "patterns of everyday life" or "sets of assumptions and ideas about the world" to which we say the children have been exposed. Before explaining what we mean by these references, we should make clear what we do not mean. We are not referring to the children's behavior as "adjustments" that they make in order to "cope" with extraordinary features of their lives, such as the inability to hear. We do not see Vicki's, Howard's or Sam's everyday signing activity with their families as an adjustment to not hearing, nor do we see their sign language as a compensation for the fact that they do not hear. "Adjustments" are what take place later in Deaf children's lives, when they arrive at school and find that their home practices are different from those of the new environment. They are startled to encounter a different set of beliefs, and must adjust to them. They must learn an alternative definition for "deaf," and new ways of interacting with the adults in their schools.

Instead, what we have been referring to are the more basic patterns of interpretation that lead Sam to ask his mother about the curious people next door, or that keep a child like Joe, who hears, from realizing he is different in any way from his Deaf family. A simple characterization of these behaviors in terms of "deafness" is not helpful, for stories like those of Sam and Joe are not unusual if compared to the way *all* children learn about the world.

Our explanation of this phenomenon is influenced by the work of theorists such as Clifford Geertz (1973), who characterizes the human being as an "unfinished animal" dependent on worlds of significant symbols. In Geertz's terms, the special condition of human beings is that their behaviors are guided by, indeed are dependent on, the presence of significant arrangements of symbols, which he calls "culture." The human capacity for culture appears over an astonishing range of specific symbol systems or "cultures." Each culture prescribes "a set of control mechanisms—plans, recipes, rules, instructions . . . for the governing of behavior" (1973:44).

By definition, cultures are highly specific systems that both explain things and constrain how things can be known. Sam wondered why the girl next door behaved so strangely. His mother offered a sensible explanation: the girl had some significantly different feature that led her to behave unlike us. Sam found this explanation completely sensible. And conversely, cultures limit the capacity to know. Howard never knew he was "deaf" until he started school; his family life did not prepare him for the odd definitions of "deaf" he would later encounter. His is not a story about failing to understand the meaning of deafness, but a story of cultural difference.

This concept of culture also explains Joe's supposedly naive ideas about himself. Joe should retrieve a fork that has fallen to the floor because eating utensils that disappear from the table should be placed back on the table; the fact that they make a sound when they fall is incidental. In Jim's hearing family, forks that fall to the floor and make a sharp noise upon contact require a look in the direction of the noise, followed by retrieval of the fork. We do not know what Jim's beliefs about sound are, but from his comments about lipreading we can deduce that he has correctly understood another significant feature in his family's everyday patterns—the role of speaking. His idea that the rest of his family have superior lipreading skills follows from his knowledge that in his family's culture interaction is crucially based on speaking.

We have used these particular examples to highlight a central point. The stories tell us not about "childish" or "naive" views of the world, but rather about the unfolding of the human symbolic capacity. Children spend their time learning what things are supposed to mean and how to think about relationships between events. As children living in the world of their caretakers, they are powerfully guided by the conventions of their culture. From the stories we have included here, we see the different ways the "recipes" and "instructions" of their worlds guide the perceptions and theories of children like Vicki, Joe, and Jim.

But here we want to focus on the similarities between the early experiences of Vicki, Helen, Sam, Howard, and Joe. There are recurrent themes that underlie their stories, a foundation of meaning that does not exist by coincidence, nor by the presence of a common physical condition. What unites their cases is the fact that each has gained access to a certain cultural history, the culture of Deaf people in America.

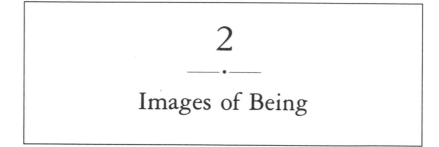

2

Images of Being

Because Deaf people as a group are not typically thought of as having been created in any one time or place, it took us a long time to recognize the following story for what it is: a folktale about the group's origins. Stories told by the members of a culture about their origins, whether they use religious or fantastic motifs, are creations of meaning about the culture's existence. They reaffirm the present by instilling meaning into the past. This particular folktale serves the same purpose—to tell where and how Deaf people began.

We had heard several stories along themes similar to the ones in this folktale, but it was not until we were displaced in a foreign country that we were able to recognize consciously what until then we had only intuitively understood: these stories are myths, tales, parables that carry the set of ideas about what makes it possible to be a Deaf person. By retelling these stories the group can talk about a knowledge it believes to be essential, its lifeblood.

We had been invited by the local Deaf club in Marseilles, France, to a specially organized dinner in our honor. Our host asked if we had heard of the Abbé de l'Epée and of how he came to meet two deaf women. We had, in fact, heard this story at the other Deaf clubs we had visited on our tour through France, but knowing that it would be impolite to refuse to watch the story, we answered that of course we would enjoy hearing it again. We settled back and once again listened to the tale of the Abbé de l'Epée, courtesy of one of the older members of the club.

The storyteller stood still for a moment to signal the beginning, then launched into a flowing performance. As we watched, we could see that his performance was almost like a recitation; it was a story that had been told many times before, but he told it with much emotion. (The language he used for the performance was not the vernacular of his community; instead he used a more gesturally based form, realizing that we were not fluent in French Sign Language.)

> The Abbé de l'Epée had been walking for a long time through a dark night. He wanted to stop and rest overnight, but he could not find a place to stay, until at a distance he saw a house with a light. He stopped at the house, knocked at the door, but no one answered. He saw that the door was open, so he entered the house and found two young women seated by the fire sewing. He spoke to them, but they still did not respond. He walked closer and spoke to them again, but they failed again to respond. The Abbé was perplexed, but seated himself beside them. They looked up at him and did not speak. At that point, their mother entered the room. Did the Abbé not know that her daughters were deaf? He did not, but now he understood why they had not responded. As he contemplated the young women, the Abbé realized his vocation.[1]

The storyteller finished with a flourish as he portrayed the Abbé struck by a vision of his mission: to educate deaf children. He then abruptly changed the mood from poetic to conversational and began to tell us the historical details of how the Abbé's efforts led to the founding of public schools for deaf children throughout France, including the school for deaf children in Bordeaux in 1785 and the National Institute for Deaf-Mutes in Paris in 1794. And he told us, as we of course had heard, that the

1. Translated by Carol Padden and Tom Humphries.

Abbé was the inventor of their beautiful signed language, a gift for which they were eternally grateful. Epée had seen that the children needed a way to communicate with one another and with their teachers, so he had devised a language of gestures for them to use.

We were curious about the emotion and reverence the story-teller showed during his recitation. Clearly the story meant a great deal to him, and though we were warmed and inspired by it, we did not fully understand why it was so important to him. We thanked him for a masterly performance, and made a mental note to read up on Epée when we returned home.

The storyteller's account of how the Abbé de l'Epée came to found a school for deaf children did not exactly fit the historical facts. The Abbé did not encounter the two deaf women as a result of a sojourn on a dark and stormy night, but instead met them on his rounds through an impoverished section of Paris. He apparently did not undergo a profound conversion experience during this encounter; instead, the idea of educating deaf children came to him after the girls' mother had asked him to give her daughters religious instruction (Lane 1976, 1984).

But there was a more significant error in our host's retelling of history. Epée did not "invent" their signed language—no individual, however gifted, can invent a human language. Instead, Epée speculated that the gestural mode of communication his students were already using before they came to his school might be an ideal channel for teaching them the French language. He explained:

> Every deaf-mute sent to us already has a language. He is thoroughly in the habit of using it, and understands others who do. With it, he expresses his needs, desires, pains, and so on, and makes no mistake when others express themselves likewise. We want to instruct him and therefore to teach him French. What is the shortest and easiest method? Isn't it to express ourselves in his language?   (Lane 1984: 59–60)

At most, the Abbé can be credited with having promoted recognition of signed language. He published numerous treatises on his educational method, which significantly incorporated the language of his students, and he became well known for his advocacy of signed language as a means for educating deaf children. Through his many public demonstrations of his deaf students' educational prowess, he increased public awareness of the existence of signed language (Lane 1976). For all his efforts, however, he was not its inventor.

So perhaps our host added a little dramatic license to a historical tale. In the spirit of storytelling, a few departures from fact would be forgivable. But there was much we did not understand about the importance of the story. Everywhere we went in France, our hosts were concerned that we not leave without hearing the tale of the Abbé de l'Epée. We wondered why they did not insist we hear other stories as well, perhaps about the founding of their local club, or about some other national figure such as Laurent Clerc. In 1814, Clerc left France to help found a school for deaf children in America—certainly a great achievement— but at the various festivities we attended, he rated only friendly toasts in the spirit of French-American cooperation, not a dramatic tale.

We finally realized that the story is not about the Abbé de l'Epée. Instead it has come to symbolize, in its retelling through the centuries, the transition from a world in which deaf people live alone or in small isolated communities to a world in which they have a rich community and language. This is not merely a historical tale, but also a folktale about the origin of a people and their language. Epée's movement from the darkness of the night into the light and warmth of the house of the deaf girls is entirely appropriate as a central image in a folktale of origins, not at all unlike folktales of other cultures.

———•———

It is not surprising that the earliest story the French Deaf people tell about themselves is a story about turning darkness into light.

The light, or the beginning, is with the first great community of Deaf people, which is said to have developed around the school the Abbé founded. From Harlan Lane's description of the years 1771–1800, it is clear that the appearance of public schools for deaf children drastically changed their social world (Lane 1984). In a translation of the childhood recollections of Jean Massieu, a deaf man who wrote an autobiographical sketch in 1798, we have a picture of how most deaf children in France lived before the establishment of schools for them:

> I was born at Semens in the Cadillac district of the canton of Saint-Macaire in the Gironde. There were six deaf-mutes in our family, three boys and three girls. Until the age of thirteen years and nine months, I remained at home without ever receiving any education. I was totally unlettered. I expressed my ideas by manual signs or gestures. At that time the signs I used to express my ideas to my family were quite different from the signs of educated deaf-mutes. Strangers did not understand us when we expressed our ideas with signs, but the neighbors did.   (Lane 1984:19)[2]

Massieu's life as the youngest of six deaf siblings was probably unlike those of most deaf children, in that he had deaf companions. Incidence rates of deafness suggest that most deaf children lived in villages in which there were no other deaf children. The appearance of public schools for the deaf brought such children together with other deaf children and deaf adults, and increased the size of their social world significantly.

More important, the schools also generated a stability that outlasted a student's school years. Many graduates remained close to the school, living in the same neighborhood. Some took jobs at the school as well, as did Massieu, who became a teacher at the same school he had attended. Today, in most cities in France where there are schools for deaf children, there are also social clubs founded by Deaf people. In Albi, for example, the club-

---

2. Translated by Harlan Lane and Frank Philip.

house for adults is across the street from the school, and the club and the school regularly use each other's facilities.

The presence of schools for deaf children created a structure that has provided a sense of continuity to the community for over two hundred years. Each new generation of children entering any one of the schools established by Epée or one of his disciples inherited a history, passed down in the school and in the community organized around the school.

While the folktale of Epée is a story about the creation of this community, it also recognizes the special circumstances of the people, that they must find one another within the world of others. Most are born into families that do not know of the community of Deaf people. Until they are somehow delivered to the school or the community around it, they cannot join the group, nor can they learn its history. Epée's wanderings along a dark road represent each deaf child's wanderings before he or she, like Epée, finds Deaf people. In every child is a Massieu, waiting to be delivered to a community and to be taught its language, or what Massieu calls "the signs of educated deaf-mutes." At the end of this quest, as at the end of Epée's search, is succor in the warmth of the community.

———— • ————

The tale of Epée is a part of American, as well as French, folk mythology. For American Deaf people, too, it symbolizes the transition from an undesirable state of being—without the community or the language—to a desirable state. One particularly emotional example appears in a letter to the editor of the *American Annals of the Deaf and Dumb* written by J. J. Flournoy, a Deaf man whom we will reintroduce in a later chapter. In a rallying cry against ignorance, Flournoy evokes almost exactly the same images seen in the French folktale: "We are not beasts, for all our deafness! We are MEN! The Era of De l'Epée has been the epocha of our birth of mind. After a long night of wandering, our planet has at length attained an orbit round a central luminary" (Flournoy 1858c:149–150).

The American Deaf community also has its own folktales, which reveal the same urge to reconstruct and affirm the community through myth that we saw in the tale of Epée. An example is the story of Joshua Davis, which originated as a family anecdote about the escapades of a relative during the Civil War but by now has had fairly wide circulation in some parts of the country. Here is one version, the one recorded in *Deaf Heritage* (Gannon 1981):

> Eighteen-year-old Joshua Davis was squirrel hunting one day on his parents' southern plantation near Atlanta, Georgia during the Civil War. Suddenly he found himself surrounded by Union soldiers. Davis was deaf but he could tell that they were shouting at him . . . Davis pointed to his ears and gestured that he was deaf but the soldiers did not believe him. They suspected that he was a spy and was trying to fool them by pretending to be deaf. They shoved and pushed the youth to a nearby house where a couple standing in front of it informed them that the youth was their son and that he was, indeed, deaf. The captors did not believe them either and they were looking for a rope to hang young Davis as a spy when a mounted officer rode up. The officer was informed that they had caught a spy who was "playing deaf." The officer rode over to the youth and fingerspelled to him: "Are you deaf?" The youth responded in signs, "Yes." "Where were you educated?" the officer asked next to which the young man told him at the school for the deaf in Cave Spring. With that information, the officer ordered the youth's release and the family's house spared.   (Gannon 1981:9–10)

The officer, as it turns out, had a deaf brother who "had taught him to talk with his hands."

In all the different versions of this story, its core is the same: a hapless Deaf boy, captured by soldiers and about to be hanged as a spy, is saved by an officer who has a Deaf relative. What distinguishes this particular version is its clever internal structure. Joshua Davis first tries to get out of his terrible predicament by using gestures: "Davis pointed to his ears and gestured that he was deaf." When this does not succeed, his parents deliver spoken pleas "that the youth was their son and that he was, indeed, deaf," but speech also fails. Then, by a stroke of providence, an officer appears and gives the boy a test. The officer fingerspells to Davis, and finds that he can respond appropriately. Next the officer asks for special knowledge that a Deaf person would have: Where was he educated? Davis again answers appropriately. Having passed the test and proved that he is Deaf, Davis goes free.

In *Deaf Heritage* the heading for this story reads, "Sign Language Saves a Life." Indeed, but the story also tells what one cannot count on to save one's life: gestures or speech. Relying on primitive gestures, one could very well find oneself hanged. Speech is likewise useless for saving a Deaf person's life. It is the special knowledge gained from other Deaf people that can save one's life.

———— • ————

Stories like these are much more than capsules of family history; they are active ways of affirming basic beliefs of the group. The stories are "instructions," which go beyond simply recalling the past and teach about how one's life should be conducted and what must be valued. Another variation of such instruction appears in a lecture entitled "Preservation of the Sign Language," delivered in 1913 by George Veditz, a former president of the National Association of the Deaf—but instead of a lesson learned from one's family, this lecture is a call to arms. Preserved on film, Veditz's lecture recalls the tale of the Abbé de l'Epée, and true to the mythology, repeats the misrepresentation of Epée's achievement:

> Friends and fellow deaf mutes . . . The French deaf people loved Epée. Every year on the occasion of his birthday they gather together at banquets and festivities to show their appreciation that this man was born on this earth. They travel to his gravesite in Versailles and place flowers and

green wreaths on his grave to show their respect in his remembrance. They loved him because he was their first teacher, but they loved him more for being the father and inventor of their beautiful sign language.[3]

The occasion for this lecture, Veditz tells us, is the thirty-third anniversary of the 1880 World Conference for the Deaf in Milan, Italy, an event that has wide circulation in popular history. In Veditz's time, as today, the conference was best remembered for the sweeping "reforms" that followed it—the banning in schools throughout Europe of signed language as a means for educating deaf children, and the new fervor directed to what Veditz calls the "oral method." The shift reflected an abandonment of the legacy of the Abbé de l'Epée; hence Veditz's allusion to Epée at the beginning of his lecture.

In recalling the Milan conference and reviling those who threatened to carry out the same reforms in American schools, Veditz calls forth vivid images:

> For the last thirty-three years, the French Deaf people have watched with tear-filled eyes and broken hearts this beautiful language of signs snatched away from their schools. For the last thirty-three years, they have striven and sought to reinstate signs in the schools, but for thirty-three years their teachers have cast them aside and refused to listen to their pleas. But their teachers would much rather listen to the worthless cruel-hearted demands of people who think they know all about educating the Deaf but know nothing about their thoughts and souls, their feelings, desires, and needs. It is like this in Germany also. The German Deaf people and the French Deaf people look up at us American Deaf people with eyes of jealousy. They look upon us Americans as a jailed man chained at the ankles might look upon a man free to wander at will. They freely admit that the American Deaf people are superior to them in matters of intelligence and spirituality, in their success in the world, in happiness.

3. Translated by Carol Padden.

And they admit that this superiority can be credited to what? . . . to one thing: that we permit the use of signs in our schools. The French Deaf people base their inferiority on one thing: the fact that oralism must be taught in their schools . . . They have eliminated fingerspelling. They have eliminated sign.

We should note here that the picture Veditz paints of the situation of Deaf Europeans is unnecessarily harsh, and that he exaggerates the contrast between Europe and America. He professes American superiority not only over European Deaf people but over their languages as well. Despite the fact that many schools for deaf children in Europe prohibited the use of sign by deaf students, signed languages in Europe did not disappear, but simply moved out of the public sphere into private areas out of the official control of schools. The communities themselves did not disintegrate as a result of changes in their ties to the schools, as evidenced by the continued presence of Deaf clubs and the schools' limited connection with them.

But, as Lane (1984) argues in his documentation of changes in Europe after the Milan Conference, there were significant shifts in political and public policy. In most schools, following the new educational edict, Deaf teachers were fired or relegated to non-teaching roles. Even before this, Deaf adults had had only a minor role in the education of deaf children, and now their contribution became even more limited.

The powerlessness of the European Deaf people against these reforms frightened Americans like Veditz. Toward the end of his speech, Veditz increases the pace of his signing as he warns of attempts to pattern American schools for deaf children after those in Europe.

But we American Deaf are rapidly approaching some bad times for our schools. False prophets are now appearing with news to the people that our American means of educating the Deaf are all wrong. These men have tried to educate people and make people believe that the oral method is really the one best means of educating the Deaf. But we

American Deaf know, the French Deaf know, the German Deaf know that in truth, the oral method is the poorest. Our beautiful sign language is now beginning to show the results of their attempts. They have tried to banish signs from the schoolroom, from the churches, and from the earth. Yes, they have tried, so our sign language is deteriorating . . . "A new race of pharaohs that knew not Joseph" are taking over the land and many of our American schools. They do not understand signs, for they cannot sign. They proclaim that signs are worthless and of no help to the Deaf. Enemies of the sign language, they are enemies of the true welfare of the Deaf . . . As long as we have Deaf people on earth, we will have signs . . . It is my hope that we all will love and guard our beautiful sign language as the noblest gift God has given to Deaf people.

Through a skillful weaving of powerful symbols, Veditz guides the viewer from the image of the good world of the Abbé de l'Epée, where signed language is ideally integrated into the community of Deaf people, to a more sinister world where the "cruel-hearted" have "snatched" their language away from them. If signed language is "snatched away" from Deaf people, they can only fall into despair, "chained at the ankles" and imprisoned as they watch others "free to wander at will," their language intact.

A modern example of this same theme of struggle in worlds proposed by others can be found in a scene from *My Third Eye,* a production of the National Theatre of the Deaf (1973). This particular scene, memorable for its brutal images, evolved out of a cast member's experience of watching a classmate being punished at a residential school. For the generation of Deaf people who attended such schools, the scene brings back memories of punishment by dunking and caning, methods that were not unusual in these schools. The actors forge a message out of what must be, for some members of the audience, an emotional link to their past.

The scene opens and we are introduced to a dimly lit stage. In a spotlight, we see a young woman held fast by two strong attendants. Behind her rises a stern and ominous figure, perhaps eight feet high, in a dark flowing robe. The attendants look at the figure as if awaiting instructions. The figure pronounces a word which the young woman is forced to repeat, but she cannot pronounce it correctly. The figure coldly gives a signal; the attendants tighten their grip and dunk her face into an unseen bowl of water. She struggles but cannot escape the strong arms of her attendants. They again dunk her in water, releasing her only when she is nearly drowned. Again the figure pronounces the word. Weakened from repeated dunkings and helpless to escape, she tries once again but again fails, again the signal and again the dunking. In the background we see the other actors standing silently by, watching a nearly drowned woman. The scene ends with the woman near death.[4]

The symbolic content of these images should be obvious at this point. Forced to speak, which she cannot do to the satisfaction of cruel and omnipotent powers, and unable to escape, the woman is consigned to a terrible death. In the story of Joshua Davis, speech, which belongs to others, cannot save the Deaf boy from death; he is saved by the grace of signed language. In Veditz's lecture we see the same contrast: on the one hand, images of imprisonment at the hands of those who insist on speech, and on the other, signed language, "the noblest gift God has given to Deaf people."

———— • ————

These stories, speeches, and performances are warnings about worlds where one falls into darkness, nonexistence, and despair. What we see in all these texts is the formulation and expression of ideas that Deaf people hold to be true and immutable. The ingredients for achieving the desirable world are the same: signed language and the shared knowledge of Deaf people, or what Veditz calls "their thoughts and souls, their feelings, desires, and needs."

4. This scene was not included in a videotape made of the production but has been reconstructed from the recollections of the actors.

The choice of images that portray bleakness, imprisonment, and death, and the association of them with a world not designed by Deaf people but proposed by others, are not accidental, but are actively built into stories like these. One way the knowledge of group members about how to conduct themselves and how to make lives for themselves is passed on is through the telling of stories about "wrong" or "dangerous" ways to live. The pressures and tensions of their everyday lives—lives spent among others who historically have been insistent that speech, not signed language, should prevail—become incorporated into their images. The group's tales about how to live without being "imprisoned," "hanged," or "drowned" are not only exhortations for protecting their own particular signed language, but also for protecting the very existence of a signed language and of their way of life in the face of tremendous pressure for speech and for living in terms of others' world.

Stories like the ones we recount here and in later chapters are essential to Deaf culture in two respects. First, as in other cultures, they are carriers of history, ways of repeating and reformulating the past for the present. And second, in the special circumstances of the Deaf community, these stories take on another burden: they are a vital means of teaching the wisdom of the group to those who do not have Deaf families. As we mentioned earlier, the incidence of deafness-causing illnesses and genetic transmission of the trait across generations is low enough that a large proportion of the community is made up of members who must learn about the culture outside of their families. The special and specific knowledge of the community, the kind of knowledge parents usually pass on to their children, must somehow be imparted by other means.

Whether these stories take the form of the political (*My Third Eye*, Veditz's speech), the ritual (the Epée story), or the romanticized (the Joshua Davis story) makes little difference. In all these cases the message they transmit from generation to generation is the same: there are ways of being Deaf.

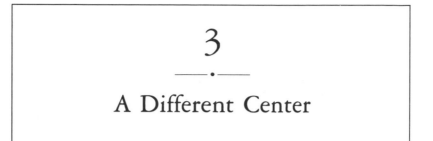

3

A Different Center

In Chapter 1 we quoted our friend Howard, who said "I never knew I was deaf until I went to school." Howard's statement shows that the meanings of DEAF and "deaf" are, at the very least, not the same. DEAF is a means of identifying the group and one's connection to it, and "deaf" is a means of commenting on one's inability to speak and hear. During a conversation with another friend, we began to understand that behind the two supposedly straightforward terms "deaf" and DEAF lie worlds of meaning that are rarely described.

The subject was whether a mutual acquaintance could use the telephone. She couldn't use the phone, our friend told us, because she was only "A-LITTLE HARD-OF-HEARING." We understood this to mean that the woman could hear only a little, not well enough to use the telephone.

On another occasion, another Deaf friend brought up the name of a woman we did not know, and explained that she had many of the recognizable characteristics of a person who could hear well, because she was VERY HARD-OF-HEARING. Our friend added that this woman regularly used the telephone to conduct business.

At the time, we did not recognize the conversations as strange; we did not think about the fact that these ASL terms, if translated literally into English, would mean the opposite of what they mean in English. Instead of using A-LITTLE HARD-OF-HEARING to mean someone whose hearing is only slightly impaired, and VERY HARD-OF-HEARING to mean someone who doesn't hear well, we and our friends used the signs to express exactly the opposite of their English meanings.

It was not until much later, when an older member of our community, Dan, asked if we realized that the signs A-LITTLE HARD-OF-HEARING and VERY HARD-OF-HEARING were being used incorrectly by some Deaf people, that we began to understand. Dan offered an explanation for these "errors": he said they were the kinds of mistakes Deaf people are inclined to make because they lack skill in the English language. We were not surprised by the explanation; at one time it would probably have occurred to us to say the same thing. Deaf people cannot hear English, so they learn it imperfectly. In this case, it was simply a matter of getting the meanings backward. Deaf people ought to be made aware of these kinds of incorrect uses of signs, Dan told us.

But if they were mistakes, we wondered, why did so many Deaf people, including those fluent in English, use them in this way? Perhaps these were not errors at all, but simply a different set of meanings. Signs from ASL are often thought to be direct representations of spoken words, but in fact they are independent of English. Although signs and their translations may have overlapping meanings, signs are not simply codes for English words. We told Dan he should describe signs in terms independent of the English words used to translate them.

But Dan was ready with his next argument. Surely we had noticed that not all Deaf people use the terms in the "wrong" way. Some, in fact many, Deaf people use the signed phrase A-LITTLE HARD-OF-HEARING to mean a person who can hear quite well and VERY HARD-OF-HEARING for someone who cannot hear well at all. What explanation did we have for that? We had to agree that these terms were also being used according to the "correct" English definitions.

Faced with two opposite sets of meanings, Dan decided that the way to resolve the contradiction was to assign a "correct" definition for HARD-OF-HEARING, and for that he chose the one that conformed to the English meaning. The other use of the term was simply incorrect in his eyes, and no amount of arguing could sway him. There must be one official definition, and any others must be simply wrong.

Our first clue to an explanation for these backward definitions came from a story another friend told us. At a football game between two Deaf schools, he saw members of the home team refer to the opposing team as HEARING. Even though the name of the opponents' school was prominently displayed on the scoreboard, the home team had strangely "forgotten" that the opponents were also Deaf. We exchanged laughs. But it occurred to us that this "error" brought out a key concept in defining HEARING: HEARING means the opposite of what we are.

The sign HEARING has an official English translation, "can hear," but in ASL HEARING is aligned in interesting ways with respect to DEAF and HARD-OF-HEARING. In ASL, as in English, HARD-OF-HEARING represents a deviation of some kind. Someone who is A-LITTLE HARD-OF-HEARING has a smaller deviation than someone who is VERY HARD-OF-HEARING. In this way, ASL and English are similar—and yet the terms have opposite meanings in the two languages. The reason for this is clear: for Deaf people, the greatest deviation is HEARING.

This is the crucial element in understanding these "backward" definitions: there is a different center, a different point from which one deviates. In this case, DEAF, not HEARING, is taken as the central point of reference. A-LITTLE HARD-OF-HEARING is a small deviation from DEAF, and thus is used for someone who is only slightly hearing. VERY HARD-OF-HEARING is someone who departs from the center greatly, thus someone who can hear quite well.

Once we had noticed the different meanings, we began to watch how these terms were used. Many of our friends, like us, did not use one definition exclusively, but often switched meanings according to context and situation. The switching never seemed awkward or confusing, but was normal and expected; the shifts were unconscious. Until our friend brought them to our attention, we had never thought about how we used the terms.

These definitions of DEAF and HARD-OF-HEARING are not remarkable and isolated examples, but are indications of a larger world of meaning where there are conventions for describing relationships between conditions and identities. Within this world of meaning—compared to that of English and the world of others—there is a different alignment, toward a different center.

———— • ————

We knew from our conversations with friends and colleagues that these labels and definitions and many more that Deaf people give themselves and others would compose a rich area of study, one often overlooked in favor of "official" or literal English meanings. When we began writing this book, people often asked us about whose lives we would describe. One friend asked if we would only write about our professional friends, or if we would also include "the average Deaf person." He reminded us that there were a lot of "average Deaf people" out there and we couldn't write only about "exceptional" Deaf people. Not all Deaf people were like us, and he wanted us to be sure to address the problems of those victimized by poor education.

Another friend, testing us, asked if we planned to write about "peddlers," the itinerant vendors who make a living by selling tokens and alphabet cards in exchange for donations. Would our book be about only the "hard-working, honest Deaf person," he asked with a hint of irony, or about all Deaf people, including the seamier types? Other friends suggested we write a book that would set "a good example" to the "hearing world" by focusing on "the intelligent Deaf."

Each recommendation, each label, points to a group within the central category of DEAF, but more clearly to us, the recommendations taken together reveal a rarely described world of meaning used by people who refer to themselves as DEAF. As we began to sort out the different categories, we focused not so much on who was in each category as on how each category was used as a way of talking about the self and about relationships with other people.

Some of the labels we came across are not used to establish commonality, but are used to label certain people as having lesser status—to marginalize them. To ignore the ways that Deaf people use a variety of labels, those which mock and tease as well as those which praise and respect, not only would paint an overly romantic picture but would make our description less rich. Each label, however petty or harsh some might seem, in its own way helps us to understand the group's deep beliefs and fears.

We started with what seemed to be the most straightforward distinction, that between DEAF and HEARING. What is DEAF? DEAF is first and foremost the group's official name for itself. Deaf organizations take care to specify "of the Deaf" in their names, as in the American Athletic Association of the Deaf, the National Fraternal Society of the Deaf, and the National Association of the Deaf (NAD). These official names contrast with that of an organization recently founded to meet the needs of adults who have lost their hearing at later ages: Self-Help for the Hard of Hearing (SHHH). Although this group's membership includes people who are deaf, its social and political agenda is distinctly different from those of the other organizations. A look at the programs for recent national conventions makes the differences clear. The NAD regularly features workshops on sign language, on improving the image of Deaf people in the media, and on how to lobby for local social service agencies "of, by and for the deaf." In contrast, SHHH offers workshops on promising new medical treatments for hearing impairment, on improving lipreading skills, and on how to use assistive devices such as amplifiers. Although in recent years the term "hearing impaired" has been proposed by many in an attempt to include both Deaf people and other people who do not hear, Deaf people still refer to themselves as DEAF.

A chance meeting with a Deaf acquaintance on the San Francisco subway (the BART) told us something about what DEAF is not. After the usual greetings, we began to make conversation: Did he work in San Francisco? Did he enjoy riding the subway? He did, and he told us he always rode the Bart because he could take advantage of a "handicapped" discount that made the sub-way much cheaper than driving to work. But then, quickly, he added, "I don't like using this disabled discount." We nodded sympathetically, and he continued, "But, hey, they offered it to me anyway, and look at how much money I'm saving." We congratulated him on his effective use of public funds. But we took note of his uneasiness and understood that for him the term "disabled" describes those who are blind or physically handi-capped, not Deaf people.

"Disabled" is a label that historically has not belonged to Deaf people. It suggests political self-representations and goals un-familiar to the group. When Deaf people discuss their deafness, they use terms deeply related to their language, their past, and their community. Their enduring concerns have been the preser-vation of their language, policies for educating deaf children, and maintenance of their social and political organizations. The mod-ern language of "access" and "civil rights," as unfamiliar as it is to Deaf people, has been used by Deaf leaders because the public understands these concerns more readily than ones specific to the Deaf community. Knowing well the special benefits, economic and otherwise, of calling themselves disabled, Deaf people have a history, albeit an uneasy one, of alignment with other disabled groups. But as our friend on the subway reminded us, "disabled" is not a primary term of self-identification, indeed it is one that requires a disclaimer.

———— • ————

Our friend's uneasiness brought us back to an earlier debate among Deaf people about how they should represent themselves to others. Beginning during World War II, Deaf organizations and political leaders began to complain of an alarming increase in the number of deaf peddlers who were soliciting donations from the public. Although deaf peddlers have existed at least since biblical times, these organizations made it clear that peddling by these "able-bodied louts" would no longer be tolerated by "hon-est and hard-working" Deaf people.

An older member of the community used the sign BEGGING

when he talked about peddlers, but technically, to avoid vagrancy laws, peddlers do not beg but sell inexpensive tokens in exchange for "contributions." After the war years, they sold packets of adhesive bandages with small cards explaining that they were deaf and had trouble finding jobs and feeding themselves and their families. The backs of the cards characteristically had an illustration of the manual alphabet with a short note: "Learn to Communicate with the Deaf!" After the war, railroad stations and downtown bars were favorite places for peddlers. A dime or a quarter was the usual contribution; on a good day, a peddler could make between $25 and $30. Peddlers still make their rounds today, but popular wisdom has it that they are "heavily into drugs." Their places of operation have been upgraded to airports and shopping malls, and they sell not bandages but combs, pens, scissors, or religious bookmarks.

The debate about peddlers probably reached its highest and most emotional point after the war. Along with the subject of sign language, a frequent topic in columns and letters to the editor in popular Deaf newsmagazines was the "problem" of peddlers. Arthur L. Roberts, the president of the National Fraternal Society of the Deaf ("The Frat"), wrote relentlessly against peddlers in the organization's publication. In one editorial he wrote: "Tell citizens they should refuse to contribute a cent to these able-bodied louts who ride around the country in good automobiles, stay at good hotels, 'work' only a few hours daily, and ridicule the gullibility of the public which supports them with their ill-gotten means of livelihood" (Roberts 1948). Roberts also made attempts to confront peddlers personally, including posting a list of names of alleged peddlers in the local Deaf club hall. The hearing son of a reputed "king" peddler, an attorney, threatened to sue him for libel and the list was removed.

The NAD established a Committee for the Suppression of Peddling, and in its official publication, the *Silent Worker*, invited readers to offer suggestions for "wiping out peddlers." Occasionally a minority voice was printed, decrying the leaders for their vicious campaigns:

How I wish Mr. [Arnold] Daulton and his committee for the suppression of peddling could come down to Arkansas and get a glimpse of the number of unemployed here—men with mouths to feed and no money to feed them with. I just don't have it in my heart to condemn these men when, after months of struggling with their conscience, they take to peddling. I have been loud in my protests against peddling, but I know that to solve a problem you must get to the root of it. Get our Arkansas peddlers jobs! I'll bet my last nickel there wouldn't be any peddling in our town then.　(Collums 1950).

The Frat and the NAD, with their new leaders, wanted a visible social and political agenda, and a crackdown on peddling was consistent with their beliefs about how to improve the lives of Deaf people. They believed that Deaf people's economic difficulties stemmed from a public image of them as lazy and ineffective. Each Deaf person was individually responsible for maintaining an appropriate image to the public. Roberts firmly believed that eliminating peddlers would also eliminate the larger society's perception that Deaf people were beggars.

A play set in a fictitious Deaf club, *Tales from a Clubroom* (Bragg and Bergman 1981), brings to the surface the tensions revealed by the controversy about peddling. The club's members snipe about a "flashy well-dressed" peddler who comes to their socials and acts as if he is one of them. But the peddler has a ready answer for those who accuse him of not getting a job and of stealing from the "hearies": "You accuse me of stealing money? Who, me? No, you're wrong. I'm only taking back what hearing people took from me because I'm deaf" (Bragg and Bergman 1981:113). Whatever the justification raised for peddling, it is counter to the way most Deaf people see themselves or want others to see them.

———— • ————

Peddlers are drawn from the ranks of what is often referred to as "the average deaf person." Leo Jacobs, in *A Deaf Adult Speaks Out* (1974), identifies nine categories of deaf people: the average deaf adult, prelingually deaf adults who come from deaf families, other prelingually deaf adults, low-verbal deaf adults, uneducated deaf adults, products of oral programs, products of public schools, deafened adults, and hard-of-hearing adults.

The first category is an important one for Jacobs. In English one might say "I'm just your average American," but in ASL the phrase "average deaf person" does not have the same quality of normality; instead it suggests someone "simple" or lacking in knowledge of the world. Deaf people who are competent in the English language and have a reasonably good knowledge of others' world are not "average" but "educated." Jacobs rails against the victimization of Deaf people that has resulted in a large group of those called "average," those who suffer because of ignorance, poor education, or poor childrearing practices. The term acknowledges the common belief that the average deaf person is more likely than not to have been victimized in this way.

The label L-V ("low-verbal") is used for educational unfortunates, but often also as a blanket term for low-income ethnic minorities. A common alternative term for L-V is "not smart." Jacobs describes these people as having "missed for various reasons a great deal of education that they should have received," so that they are almost illiterate. When we once inquired about attending a Deaf club in an urban area, we were told that we would not find it useful to go because members of the club were mostly L-V. Carol was told as a child that many Deaf peddlers were L-V, manipulated into working for unscrupulous king peddlers. More informal terms include, loosely translated, "those out of it," "locals," and "those who do drugs." Again, although these distinctions primarily refer to educational features, they are ways of labeling the uneducated, the working poor, and the chronically unemployed.

With his use of the term "prelingually," Jacobs acknowledges the official distinctions others use for the Deaf population. Those who "lost their hearing before the acquisition of language" are called "prelingually" Deaf, while "postlingually" Deaf is used for those who lost their hearing after having acquired "language." "Language" in this sense, of course, is used to mean English, not sign language. The distinction ignores those who have learned sign language as a first language, and who hence are native users of a human language, like those who are "postlingually deaf." The terms, as would be expected within an official frame with HEARING at the center, emphasize the role of onset of hearing loss and the presence of English, rather than the age at which any human language, including ASL, is acquired.

But Jacobs modifies this distinction and incorporates another; working around the official frame, he adds a new category: "prelingually deaf adults who come from deaf families." He writes that members of this category are "more outgoing and at ease with other deaf persons" and are less likely to have feelings of inferiority. "Other prelingually deaf adults," that is, those who do not have deaf families, form "the bulk of the deaf community," and "come from hearing families who have had trouble communicating with them when they were little." Jacobs adds the unfair generalization that "they are for the most part less aggressive and confident" than those "prelingually deaf adults who come from deaf families" (1974:56–57).

———— • ————

Deaf children of Deaf parents may have a respected status among Deaf people because they display effortless facility in the language of the group. But like all the distinctions we have been discussing, this one is not simple. For one thing, outside the group, the notion that parents knowingly gave birth to children when there was a good possibility that the children might be deaf is not an acceptable one. This opinion of others has insidiously affected the way Deaf people view their own Deaf children. On the one hand they are respected and on the other stigmatized.

Out of this deep contradiction, the two groups, Deaf children of Deaf families and Deaf children of hearing families, play out their public images and respond to this tension in different ways. The husband of a Deaf couple told us that for a long time he harbored feelings of superiority over his wife when he introduced himself as having lost his hearing in childhood. His wife, on the other hand, introduced herself as having Deaf parents. By explaining that he had lost his hearing, he could avoid the silent condemnation he believed hearing people directed toward his wife, who had inherited her deafness. He himself could not be held responsible for his condition because he had become deaf "by accident," that is, through illness.

Stories we have heard about hearing children born to Deaf families also involve conflicting sentiments that reveal the complexity of the rules for categorization and identity. For example, a friend told us about a recent dispute at a local Deaf basketball club over a hearing son of Deaf parents who wanted to play for the club. Because this young man could hear, he would have been automatically barred from playing in any games sanctioned by the American Athletic Association of the Deaf (AAAD). Sports organizations like these are one of the few places where Deaf people exercise almost total control over their own affairs, from deciding their own rules to determining who qualifies as a member. And one of the inviolable rules is that hearing players cannot play, on grounds of "unfair" competition. But in this particular case, the club's officers wavered and delayed action that would have removed the player. When the officers of the regional organization learned that the club had a player who was not "legally" Deaf, they pressed the club to act. Recognizing that the hearing player was in all other respects a member of the group, behaved as a Deaf person, and was virtually indistinguishable from his teammates, the club tried labeling him HARD-OF-HEARING. When the regional officers insisted on an audiological test, the club's officers knew they had played their last card and regretfully asked him to leave the team.

The club probably would not have tried to violate the rules if the hearing player had not had Deaf parents. There would have been no queston of his being allowed to play. Despite the na-

tional organization's watchfulness, there are stories of other basketball clubs where "arrangements" are made allowing hearing
children of Deaf parents to play, either "illegally" or at non-
AAAD-sanctioned games. No such allowance is ever made for
genuine outsiders.

Hearing children of Deaf parents represent a special problem.
They have blood ties to Deaf people as well as knowledge of the
customs and language of the group. The club officials knew their
efforts to keep the player would be supported by the members,
and their attempt to label him HARD-OF-HEARING was a desperate but not impossible move to keep him within the category of
DEAF. When that move failed, they had no choice but to remove
him. In matters where these labels count, such as competing
fairly for a prize, the boundaries between DEAF and HEARING are
firm.

———— • ————

Real HARD-OF-HEARING people walk a thin line between being
Deaf people who can be like hearing people and Deaf people who
are too much like hearing people. They can be admired for their
ability to seem like others for specific purposes, but they are
viewed with suspicion when they begin to display behaviors of
the others when there is no apparent need to, such as when there
are no hearing people present. A friend who uses the telephone
"without effort" confided that in the presence of new Deaf ac-
quaintances she finds herself feigning difficulty on the telephone
to avoid being categorized toward the hearing end of the HARD-
OF-HEARING continuum. Another Deaf woman whose Deaf parents and friends call her HARD-OF-HEARING remembers that in
her adolescence her parents showed surprise and disbelief when
she described having problems communicating with her hearing
co-workers. "But you can hear and talk," they told her. Since she
was more like hearing people, she was not entitled to make the
kinds of complaints Deaf people use about the difficulty of communicating with hearing people.

A hard-of-hearing friend who successfully walks this line was

described as "DEAF but really HARD-OF-HEARING," an acknowl-
edgment of his ability to use his skills selectively. HARD-OF-
HEARING people can also be DEAF, but there is an imaginary
asterisk by their label, qualifying them from time to time.

The label HARD-OF-HEARING involves discussion about having
characteristics like hearing people, but being called ORAL is a
stronger accusation. A Deaf man reported that though he had no
hearing and his voice was barely intelligible, he had become used
to being called HARD-OF-HEARING because his mouthing behavior was very "hearing-like." He had lost his hearing at six years of
age and did not mind being called "deafened," but he drew the
line at being called ORAL. Because ORAL represents a misaligned
center, the results of having made wrong choices in life, it is an
unacceptable insinuation to someone who considers himself
DEAF.

The sign ORAL incorporates a long social and political history
of the role of the school in the community. "Oral" schools pro-
mote ideologies counter to those of Deaf people; "manual"
schools, which allow use of signed language in the schools, are
ideologically appealing to Deaf people. Although the term "oral"
is slowly losing its traditional context—many schools are no
longer represented as either "oral" or "manual," the labels having been replaced by newer terms such as "total communication"—it is still used to represent an ever-present threat, the
malevolent opposition.

At a conference for teachers of ASL, a woman stood before her
peers and warned that while teachers squabble among themselves
about signed language and the different "sign systems," there are
"oralists" out there hatching new plots to remove signed language from the education of Deaf children. Let us not forget our
true enemy, she proclaimed.

ORAL recalls many extreme stereotypes; our friends gave us
two: MIND RICH and ALWAYS PLAN. ORAL individuals are stereo-
typically represented as members of the establishment, as coming
from hearing families that are inflexible about their children's
behavior. As the belief goes, the richer the family, the more

likely the family will embrace oralism (MIND RICH). The second stereotype portrays a typical ORAL person as one who actively tries to pass as hearing, and must be alert to every possible situation in order to pass successfully (ALWAYS PLAN). In its strongest connotations, ORAL means one who "cozies up to the opposition" and uncritically embraces the world of others.

ORAL FAIL ("oral failure") is a term used for those who are products of oppressive educational programs. Deaf teachers talk of having to take in "oral failures" in their "manual" classrooms, of having to take care of others' "rejects." One example appears in *A Deaf Adult Speaks Out*:

> The deaf pupils were only allowed to change to "manual classes" when they proved to be failures in the oral method, usually during their adolescence. These older pupils were generally considered to be brain damaged, aphasic or "slow" by their teachers. Thus many bright and capable youngsters were labeled failures in everything else. Thus incalculable damage was done not only to their self-image but also to their capabilities for optimum achievement toward desirable careers.   (Jacobs 1974:34)

"Oral failures" are, like ORALS, those who pay the price for wrong life choices, but they can be redeemed and become #EX ORAL. (The symbol # is a convention used to represent vocabulary borrowed from fingerspelling.) Jacobs recounts stories of "oral failures" who recover from the damage done to them in their early years and, with the help of instruction in signed language, regain their hidden abilities: "Ted found himself when he discovered manual communication, and was soon making astonishing progress. He caught up with his age level, and displayed an extraordinary bent for mathematics. His language developed at such a rate that he was writing fairly adequate English ₀at the time of his graduation from the school" (p. 36).

In *Tales from a Clubroom*, members of the club charitably call their resident oralist, Spencer Collins, an #EX ORAL because he has repented and joined their ranks. But his slow, lumbering manner remains a comfortable symbol to the others of his past and their own good luck in not being ORAL themselves.

Stories about people like Collins are popular. They are defectors from others' world, those oralists who, when they come of age and are free to make their own choices, join the world of Deaf people as adults and learn signed language. Carol remembers as a child attending an evening at a local Deaf bowling league where a friend pointed out a woman several alleys down. This woman's father was a prominent leader of oral education, the friend said, and yet here she was, mixing and signing with us like a regular. She had rebelled against her father and married a Deaf man! The defection was as significant as that of a daughter of a prominent Soviet party official. All it takes, Carol's friend explained, is a taste of our world and they want to leave the old one behind.

In fantasy storytelling, an ORAL is a powerful symbol of one in need of being rescued. At a party, a man told a variation on a Cinderella story with an impoverished ORAL girl. The simple structure of the fairy tale highlighted the idealized difference between those who are ORAL and those who are DEAF. This deaf Cinderella is given a pair of glass gloves by her fairy godmother, allowing her to sign effortlessly and gracefully. Her ragged clothing disappears under her godmother's wand, and she finds herself wearing jewelry made by Deaf artists. She goes to the Deaf club and falls in love with the son of the club president. With her glass gloves, she captivates the "prince" of the club. At midnight, true to the original story, she flees, leaving behind one of the glass gloves. The story ends as predicted: the "prince" finds the girl of his dreams, and she becomes his "princess," her magic gloves allowing her to erase her many years as an ORAL person and gain the difficult but admired skill of signing like a native.

A trendier accusation that one Deaf person can make of another, one some older members of the community find confusing, is THINK-HEARING. Its literal meaning is "to think and act like a hearing person," but a more accurate translation is "to embrace uncritically the ideology of others." The term's range of meaning is similar to that of ORAL, except that the accusation can be made against any Deaf person, including those who are not ORAL, that is, not orally trained.

THINK-HEARING illustrates the present generation's sophistication with sign structure (which we describe in Chapter 5). Instead of an adaptation of an existing sign, as with ORAL which also means SPEECH or MOVING-LIPS, THINK-HEARING is a novel creation formed by combining selected elements from the two signs THINK and HEARING (see figure 3.1). THINK-HEARING goes beyond ORAL to include other unacceptable choices such as voicing opposition to ASL, or insisting that signers should use among themselves invented sign vocabulary developed for teaching English to deaf children. Older members of the community, more comfortable with the distinction between "oral" and "manual," or between not signing and signing, find accusations based on what kind of signing one uses unfamiliar. THINK-HEARING, through its self-conscious analysis of signs, emphasizes a modern realignment of the center.

———— • ————

As we have said, to understand how these categorizations and labels work one must begin from a different center. Deaf people work around different assumptions about deafness and hearing from those of hearing people. The condition of not hearing, or of being hard of hearing, cannot be described apart from its place-

Figure 3.1

HEARING

THINK-HEARING

ment in the context of categories of cultural meaning. Names applied to one another are labels that define relationships. The relationships Deaf people have defined include their struggles with those who are more powerful than they, such as hearing others.

A person who is "DEAF but really HARD-OF-HEARING" has skillfully managed his relationships across groups. Deaf people may use a politically advantageous label such as "disabled," but they must apologize for it among themselves. Jacobs borrows the supposedly scientific distinction between "prelingually deaf" and "postlingually deaf" and adds modifiers that readjust the relationships in ways that are more compatible with group knowledge. All of these adjustments indicate how well the center accommodates and, at the same time, how tightly it holds.

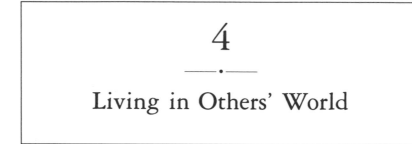

4

·

Living in Others' World

Deaf people for the most part have always lived within the world of others. Thus it is not surprising that their theories about themselves and their language are powerfully colored by beliefs held by others. The story that the Abbé de l'Epée invented signed language, for one, is a reconciliation of what Deaf people believe with what others believe. Epée's metaphorical role in the creation of their community is illustrated by the magical powers assigned to him.

If we look further at the speech by George Veditz from which we quoted in Chapter 2, we find another example of the imparting of unwarranted powers to others. Veditz gives the following account of the way signed languages are transmitted across generations:

> From olden years, the masters of this sign language, the Peets, the Dudleys, the Elys, the Ballards are rapidly disappearing, and we, in past years, loved these men. They had a precise command of the sign language, they could communicate to us using only signs and we could understand them. But fortunately, we have several masters of our sign language still with us. Edward Miner Gallaudet learned this sign language from his father, Thomas Hopkins Gallaudet. There are several others like Dr. John B. Hotchkiss, Dr. Edward Allen Fay, Robert P. MacGregor who are still with us. And we want to preserve the signs as these men now use them to keep and pass on to future generations . . . there is

but one known means of passing on the language: through the use of moving picture films.   (Veditz 1913)[1]

Veditz gives to the hearing persons he mentions the responsibility for transmitting signed language. Significantly, he neglects to credit Edward Miner Gallaudet's Deaf *mother* for her hearing son's language competence, and instead says he learned it from his father, a hearing man. Sophia Fowler Gallaudet had an older Deaf sister and a Deaf cousin who lived across the street (Gannon 1981; Lane 1984). It is likely that she was exposed to signed language at an early age, and this would suggest that Edward had a proficient model of the language in his mother, perhaps a better model than his father, who had no knowledge of any signed language until he met Laurent Clerc at the age of twenty-nine.

Veditz believed, as was customary in his time, that signed languages are derived from spoken languages and have been invented by individuals such as Epée. His repeated references to Epée and Gallaudet suggest that he thought signed language would gain prestige or respect by being associated with leading hearing figures. If such esteemed men were responsible for the language, then it could not be as primitive or as degraded as others thought. He probably also believed that languages are transmitted primarily by intellectuals rather than by any normally competent person. His urgent appeal for preserving the purity of sign language on film implies that he thought the language's survival depended on continuing the direct line of transmission from Gallaudet himself.

Veditz's ideas about signed language can be traced to predominant beliefs held by others. Here again we arrive at the problem Deaf people have of developing an independent understanding of themselves. Given that they live within the world of others, is a science about Deaf people a science of themselves or one given to them by others?

———•———

1. Translated by Carol Padden.

The problem of how to describe signed languages is not new. In his book *Language* (1921), Edward Sapir, one of the foremost linguists of this century, articulated the standard view of his time when he described signed languages of "groups of deaf-mutes" as in the same category as gestures of "Trappist monks vowed to perpetual silence" and "the gesture language of the Plains Indians of North America" (1921:21). Later, Sapir's student Leonard Bloomfield, an influential force in the field of language studies for most of this century, continued the same line of thinking: "It seems certain that these gesture languages are merely developments of ordinary gestures and that any and all complicated or not immediately intelligible gestures are based on the conveniences of speech" (1933:39).

These descriptions fail to notice two ways in which signed languages are different from gestures of monks and Plains Indians. First, signed languages are acquired as first languages, whereas the other systems are used to supplement the group's spoken language. Second, signed languages are the primary mode of social interaction for the groups that use them. Trappist monks, it is safe to assume, learned to speak before they took their vow of silence; hence their gestural systems are not primary languages but systems devised for unusual circumstances. Although the original descriptions are confused, it is clear from rereading the available records that the gestural systems of the Plains Indians were not used within a tribe as a mode of social discourse, but rather were means of communicating with other tribes who spoke different languages (Mallery 1972; Perlmutter 1986).

Sapir and Bloomfield did not examine signed languages in detail to see whether they could identify structures resembling those found in oral languages. If they had, as have a number of investigators in the present generation of scholars, they would have discovered a remarkable similarity of categories of structures (Perlmutter 1986).

Although Sapir and Bloomfield did not venture further into the description of signed languages, their authority was enough to establish the tone of official thought. For the next generation of those influential in deciding how deaf children in America would be taught, Helmer Myklebust's *Psychology of Deafness* (1957) set the standard. Speech is the basis for human language, and all other forms are derivatives:

> The manual sign language used by the deaf is an Ideographic language . . . it is more pictorial, less symbolic . . . Ideographic language systems, in comparison with verbal symbol systems, lack precision, subtlety, and flexibility. It is likely that Man cannot achieve his ultimate potential through an Ideographic language . . . The manual sign language must be viewed as inferior to the verbal as a language. (1957:241–242)

The implication for Deaf people who use signed languages is clear: their choice makes them lesser humans, unable to achieve their ultimate human potential. These beliefs were not based on an analysis of signed languages, but rather on impressionistic evidence that was allowed to take on scientific weight. The dismissive tone of Myklebust's cursory review of signed languages was not considered degrading or suspiciously researched, but became a standard.

———— • ————

In the face of the opinions of others about signed languages, what kinds of theories did Deaf people themselves develop about their language? Evidence can be found in back issues of the *Silent Worker*, a forum where Deaf people exchanged ideas about a variety of topics, frequently including their language. The *Silent Worker*, when it was revived in 1948 after nearly twenty years, rapidly became one of the most widely read magazines in the Deaf community. As part of a strategy by Byron B. Burnes, then president of the National Association of the Deaf, the magazine set out to improve the image of Deaf people by portraying them as hard-working, law-abiding citizens. (This same concern for public image later led the NAD to rename the magazine the *Deaf*

American because the older name was too close to that of the official organ of the American Communist Party, the *Daily Worker.*)

An editorial in the February 1950 issue interested us because it had preserved shades of Veditz's lecture—as children the editors had known Veditz, and his many public orations remained in their memories. The theme of the editorial picked up on Veditz's cry that the survival of sign language was threatened:

> the sign language is in danger of becoming a lost art unless something is done by the deaf to keep it at a standard where it can be considered the medium of conversation of a cultured people . . . The tendency today is away from standard usage, in favor of improvised signs and "slang" signs. If the tendency continues, the time will come when the sign language will no longer be universal, and the deaf in one state will be unable to converse freely with those of another state.   (Burnes 1950)

The editorial goes on to give a curious description of "the sign language": "There is no grammar in the sign language. There is no standard authority by which it is determined that one sign is correct and another is incorrect, but custom has given us a fairly good standard, and we recognize a correct and incorrect form of usage."

The editorial writer subscribes to a long tradition of describing his language as lacking any internal organization or structure. Indeed, it has no special name but is called simply "the sign language."

As Deaf people from a different generation, we know that because natural signed languages have been transmitted from one generation of users to the next, they are not primitive but complex systems. The fact that generations of children learn the language, thereby imposing structures and systems on it, is one kind of argument modern investigators use for grouping signed languages with other natural languages and for distinguishing them from derivative systems.

Why then did the editors of the *Silent Worker* describe their language in terms almost as dismissive as Myklebust's? We could use the same answer we came up with for Veditz's errors: it was simply unthinkable at the time to refer to signed language in the kind of terms used by modern linguists. No respectable hearing linguist in 1950 would have suggested, as linguists do today, that signed languages contain verb agreement, have rich combinatory qualities, and have dependent and independent clauses. Books about signed language published at that time consisted of only lists of signs, grouped in broad categories such as "food" and "emotions." No rules of the language were included, except for "tips" on how to use it, because it was believed there were no rules beyond a simple mapping onto English or a set of general logical principles easily discerned by the learner.

But when we looked at the *Silent Worker* editorial closely we found interesting ways of describing "the sign language." What first struck us was the reference to the language as an "art." Veditz's repeated references to signing as "beautiful," "lovely," and "graceful" were consistent with the idea of "art." This view of the language is still active today, as evidenced by a poem by Patricia Smolen (1982) that appeared in the *Silent News,* a popular deaf newspaper published monthly out of New York City:

Changing Signs
The language of signs so deeply ingrained
By deaf forebears, for years was unchanged,
Signs are being revised by the new breed
Spurred on by the hearing who don't know our need.
"For the sake of progress," it is loudly proclaimed,
Old signs are altered, a few left to remain.

We the golden agers, do sadly decry
Strange hand motions but learn them we try
The sign language once so lovely to see
Has changed to a language confusing to me.

Again, the adjective is "lovely," to describe a language constantly threatened by outside influences. In the passage from

Veditz we quoted in the beginning of this chapter, the ideal signer is a "master," an artist who is revered and loved for a "precise command" of the language. It is implied that good signing is like a beautiful painting or sculpture: there is an order in how the parts come together. The result of correct signing is aesthetically pleasing and satisfying. Bad signing, in contrast, is jarring and unpleasant. The *Silent Worker* editorial goes on to complain:

> There exists today a notable carelessness in the use of the sign language. The old-time masters of the sign language used a clear-cut, carefully chosen style of delivery which was easy to understand and pleasing to see. Today too many deaf are inclined to slur over their spelling and crowd their signs, and in order to understand them, one must strain both one's eyesight and one's mentality.   (Burnes 1950)

In the larger society that surrounds Deaf people, the typical way of referring to orderly systems like languages is as an interlocking system of rules and grammars. But Veditz and the editors of the *Silent Worker* referred to their language in terms of a different aesthetics: not of rules, but of art. Masters of the language have perfected "a clear-cut, carefully chosen style of delivery," which is "pleasing to see." And like students of art, students of the sign language would do well to study with masters. A failure to adhere to the rules (or what we would now call ungrammatical signing) "strains both one's eyesight and one's mentality." Without a notion of the grammaticality of signed language, the editors could only describe failures in competence in terms of how they "strain" the viewer.

Another example is from the *Silent Worker*'s response to a reader who had written commending a columnist for his strong position on the sign language; her concern was the sloppy declamation of "The Star-Spangled Banner." The columnist, Emerson Romero, responded: "There seems to be a feeling among many of our sign slingers that it makes little difference what sign one uses as long as it is understood. People are losing sight of the fact that there are correct signs, and a correct form of delivery, just as there is a correct form of English grammar" (Romero 1950).

What did these writers mean by "a correct form of delivery" and "a clear-cut, carefully chosen style of delivery"? What could these phrases mean but a sense of rules? What is "a precise command of the sign language" but an ability to use the grammar correctly? Contrary to the popular belief that signed languages are based on speech and derive their rules from spoken language, the *Silent Worker* editors and Veditz complain that those who do not know the language, including those who presumably know the spoken language, persist in creating unacceptable sign sentences, or, to use today's terminology, ungrammatical sentences.

———— • ————

We came across another good example of this type of complicated vocabulary in a filmed interview, *Charles Krauel: Portrait of a Deaf Filmmaker* (1986). Krauel began making home movies of various Deaf activities in 1925 and continued to make films for many years. His films are among our best surviving records of Deaf life from as early as 1925.

Krauel, interviewed at age ninety-two, was asked about his world as he filmed it and about his life today in a different generation. He reminisced about the old days when clothing, hats, and, as he added with a note of regret, even signs were different.

> Nowadays, signs are different. Back then, signs were better, you know, natural, but now with all these IS kind of signs, and all that—well, it may be good for children who need to learn language. Those kinds of signs are good language. My signs are not, they're like "short-cuts," more abbreviated. But it sure saves time though. This faster way of talking is much clearer. Nowadays, with IS and all those things, you get these long drawn-out sentences that take forever to sign. It's a waste of time, I tell you.[2]

2. Translated by Carol Padden.

Krauel is contrasting his language with recently developed pedagogical tools variously called Seeing Essential English, Signing Exact English (both of these go by the acronym SEE), or Signed English. Collectively called "manual English systems," they were created by committees of educators for the purpose of teaching English to deaf children. In these systems, new signs are invented for English words that do not have single sign translations, such as the third-person present-tense singular form of the verb "to be" ("all these IS kind of signs"). Old signs are also modified in a further attempt to impose correspondence between English and ASL. The normal order of signs in ASL is reorganized in an attempt to mirror the order of words in English sentences (Gustason and Woodward 1973). To use an example we have mentioned before, the sequence I-GIVE-HIM BOOK MAN is ungrammatical in ASL, but in an attempt to mirror the English sentence "I gave a book to a man" invented systems use this order and add invented signs to supply the "missing English elements." These attempts, however well-intentioned, rest on the pervasive belief that signed languages are essentially "incomplete" systems and amenable to modification for educational purposes. They ignore the fact that individual signs, like words, are inseparable parts of a larger grammatical system.

These kinds of violations are probably what leads Krauel to complain about "long drawn-out sentences that take forever to sign." Despite his intuitions about his language—a "faster way of talking" that "saves time" and is "natural"—Krauel explains that his language is not "good" language. Manual English, in contrast, is good for deaf children because it teaches them "language."

Krauel borrows the widely used convention of distinguishing between English and ASL by using the signs LANGUAGE (for English) and SIGN (for ASL). In this way, his vocabulary is consistent with that of official sources. In 1967 the Department of Health, Education and Welfare issued a circular entitled "Life Problems of Deaf People: Prevention and Treatment," which was widely circulated. According to the authors, Mary Switzer and

Boyce Williams, "Many Deaf people . . . have very limited language skills. They receive information mainly through the eyes. They impart information by combinations of signs, gestures, speech, and writing, although the large majority prefer signs between themselves and hearing persons who are masters of sign language" (1967). This usage carries the implication that Deaf people are unable to learn any language—an incorrect belief but one that has persisted until very recently.

Krauel has more to say about his language. As he tries to explain what he means about the difference between manual English and what he uses himself, he hesitates and is almost apologetic. Sign language is "natural," he says, implying that manual English is not. He pauses as if to ask his interviewer to understand what he means. What is he trying to say?

We think that by "natural" he means what is expected, not strange or bizarre. A human language is natural; its orderliness does not "strain both one's eyesight and one's mentality." Artificial languages, such as invented sign systems, do not have this quality; they lack the power of systems of rules created by generations of children learning from adults who themselves acquired the language as children.

Krauel's intuitive reference to his language as "abbreviated" and made up of "short-cuts" suggests that he believed it to be less than complete, but it also captures the idea that his language is an efficient system that stands in contrast to the laborious systems invented by committee, such as manual English.

With Krauel, as with Veditz and others, we see again the contradictory ways of talking about the language. Krauel says his language is not good for children, but it is natural and efficient. It doesn't have qualities associated with spoken language, but it does the kinds of things spoken languages do.

This doublespeak grows out of an attempt to reconcile two very powerful truths: signed language is rejected by the larger society, but it is the essence of how Deaf people live and how they understand their lives. Having to live with both these truths, Deaf people acknowledge the official truth by using the official vocabulary but reserve a special vocabulary for the oppositional truth, their own contrary knowledge.

———— • ————

In the play *Tales from a Clubroom* (Bragg and Bergman 1981) we can see how these competing sets of knowledge play themselves out in the social world of Deaf people. First presented at the centennial celebration of the NAD in 1980, the play has been popular as a glimpse into the everyday world of the Deaf person. A large part of the appeal of the play is its more-real-than-real characters, their types familiar to anyone who has spent much time in local Deaf clubs. Abe Green is the stereotypical rough-and-tough club president; Will Grady is the club jester and operator of the movie projector. From the time the play opens on a captioned film night at the club, to its climax, when the club treasurer is exposed for embezzling club funds, the audience can almost predict how the characters will play out their roles.

The plot is almost secondary to the way the actors personify, indeed amplify, the tensions within the Deaf community. For example, the status and styles of the characters Mark Lindsey and Tim Shalleck illustrate the ways social lines are drawn over the problem of how to talk about language.

When Mark Lindsey makes his entrance and begins to sign " 'Englishy,' that is, with English syntax," the audience chortles in anticipation of an upcoming battle. Lindsey is a graduate of Gallaudet College, a college for deaf students, and one of Smolen's "new breed" who use what Krauel called "all these IS kind of signs." At one point in the play, Lindsey is warned by Will Grady that his social class—as marked by his education and brand of signing—is going to get him in trouble with the club members:

Grady: Say, you use some strange signs.
Lindsey: What do you mean, strange?
Grady: You fingerspell big words. "Operate, opretate." I don't
    know how to fingerspell it. And you use fancy signs . . . Our

signs are good enough for us. I'm older than you, so let me give you some advice. You came here to make some new friends, right? (Lindsey nods.) If you want to be accepted, don't act like a smartass or you won't make any friends.

Tim Shalleck is everything Lindsey is not: a "muscular bartender with limited education; uses only the simplest and most picturesque signs (ASL)." Here we see a symbolic opposition between the ways the two men are described. Lindsey's signs are "fancy," but Shalleck's are "simple" and "picturesque." Lindsey is a college graduate, one of "the high-cultured" type; Shalleck is a bartender with limited education. The two characters are immediately suspicious of each other, and later, symbolically, they fight over a woman. The audience expects to see tension between them as they play out very real tensions in the community.

As we watch the other characters interact with Lindsey, we see that they do not take him entirely seriously, in fact they hold him at a distance. Grady and the others resent Lindsey's use of "fancy" signs and his repeated complaints about "lack of culture" in the club. We understand these reactions as a shared rejection by the club members of Lindsey's belief that signed language is inferior and needs to be fixed.

But Lindsey is not without influence. Other members, while they keep him in his place, sometimes mimic his style, as when the club president's wife, Mrs. Greene, uses manual English during an announcement. But Mrs. Greene apologizes for her lapse: "Excuse my sign language! My children in school are influencing my signing; I'm using SEE."

Any indulgence of Lindsey disappears, however, when tension leads to conflict. Observe the following exchange between Shalleck and Lindsey, in which Lindsey suggests that Shalleck himself, by association with the language, is inferior:

Lindsey: (Fingerspells to Shalleck) Tom Collins!
Shalleck: (Shakes his head, showing that he doesn't understand Lindsey. Yabuski talks in picture signs to Shalleck who grins

and shakes his head and points to the two bottles on the shelf.)
Don't have. First or second? . . .

Lindsey: (To Yabuski) What's the matter with this bartender?
Doesn't he read fingerspelling?

Yabuski: (To Lindsey) Shh! Be quiet.

Shalleck: (Moves angrily to Lindsey and taps him roughly on the
shoulder.) You think I'm dumb? I have a house, a wife, children and a car. What've you got?

Shalleck does not understand the English term for the mixed
drink, so Yabuski translates by using "picture signs." This term,
seemingly borrowed directly from the language in Myklebust's
textbook, is used here to suggest signed vocabulary as more
concrete, less sophisticated, and by implication inferior to
manual English. The implication is clear: Shalleck needs picture
signs because he is of low intelligence.

But Shalleck is a member of the club's board and is highly
regarded by other members. The woman Shalleck and Lindsey are
competing for prefers Shalleck, and in the final showdown Shalleck wins:

Lindsey: (To Shalleck) . . . I have news for you friend, she's a cock
tease! . . .

Shalleck: That's enough from you. Tell the lady you're sorry
or . . .

Lindsey: (To Greene) Get this gorilla away from me! Do something!

Greene: (To Lindsey) I won't permit female club members to be
insulted by outsiders. Get out! . . . You've no right to bully
and insult ladies.

Lindsey: This is between me and the lady. None of your business.

Greene: But it is our business! We look out for each other! You
have a college degree—big deal! You're no better than any of
us. We're sincere . . . We have hearts! All you have inside you
is a knife and smart aleck words!

Shalleck: (To Lindsey) Are you man enough to apologize to the
lady?

Greene: (To Lindsey) Either apologize or get out!

Lindsey: You leave me with no other choice . . . I guess I proved who's dumb.

Shalleck: (Menacingly) Who's dumb?

Just as the club members reject Lindsey but allow him to have some influence, they embrace Shalleck but say he has limitations. The audience understands the tensions between the two characters because they are important ones within the community. Signed language is honorable, but the club members seem unable to escape the suspicion that it may be what others say it is, a form inferior to human language, and worse yet, that people who use it may also be inferior. Shalleck is, after all, only a bartender.

———— • ————

All the examples we have quoted in this chapter illustrate a particular problem. The "science" of others, which celebrates speech, is so pervasive that it effectively overpowers a different knowledge, namely Deaf people's knowledge about signed language. Typically, when Deaf people portray their language as "lifesaving," as in the story about Joshua Davis (Chapter 2), their beliefs are considered "personal" or "romantic." When Veditz warns against those who would eliminate the language, his plea is counted as a "political" one. When the editors of the *Silent Worker* observe that others do not use the language correctly (for the logical reason that they have never learned its rules), this is dismissed as a complaint about "style" rather than grammar.

Others believe that Deaf people are protective and romantic about signed languages because they are "dependent" on them. Lacking the ability to use speech, it is said, they become overly sentimental about their "adaptive means." In contrast, hearing people surely do not think of themselves as "dependent," in any pejorative way, on speech.

Embedded in the texts we have presented is a complicated understanding of how signed languages work. Deaf people's writings reveal a self-analysis that is not, strictly speaking, scientific—it is impressionistic, global, and not internally analytic—but their many adjustments of theories proposed by others suggest that they find the theories of others inadequate, imbalanced, and sometimes, about the most important ideas, false. That they live with others' theories while maintaining separate theories of their own is a tribute to the powerful possibilities of their culture.

5

———·———

A Changing Consciousness

David, an older member of the Deaf community, complained to us about a questionnaire he had been asked to fill out about his early language experience. He couldn't answer the questions, he said. One question asked what language he had used at home with his Deaf parents, and listed the following choices: speech, ASL, or one of the other modes of signing. But, he told us, none of the choices was correct. We were taken aback. Why wouldn't ASL be the correct answer, since his parents were Deaf and he had used the language from birth? "But we didn't call it 'ASL' back then. We didn't call it anything, we just did it. How can I call it one of these when we didn't call it any of them?"

In David's childhood, his family had never had a specific name for what they used to communicate with one another. The activity of signing had been called simply "sign language," or "manual language"—as it was in the *Silent Worker* editorial we quoted in Chapter 4. But today there are names for different kinds of signing. The natural signed language used in the United States is called American Sign Language, or ASL; English-influenced signing has another name, Sign English; and then there are the various manual English systems, including those with pedagogically persuasive names such as Signing Exact English, or SEE.

As an adult David knew the new terminology, and could use it himself to talk about his own signing or that of others. Perhaps what distressed him about the questionnaire was that the names connote certain histories that he would have to weigh in his answer.

If he called the language he used at home ASL—the answer we expected him to choose—he might find himself accused of having an impoverished language background by those who believe ASL is inferior to English. As a Deaf man who had learned English well, he found such a suggestion offensive. He was no Tim Shalleck, no simple bartender, but a professional member of his community.

His reluctance to rename something familiar, even taken for granted, is understandable. The term "ASL" implies a particular history, one he was not sure he wanted to adopt. The best solution, he told us, was just to call it "the sign language," as he always had. But this choice was not listed. The new generation has names for what David and his contemporaries thought of as "just something we did." There are several possible names for the entire activity of signing, and the choice one makes among them depends not only on what type of activity one is referring to but also on its social and political implications.

These new tensions inspired Gilbert Eastman's *Sign Me Alice* (1974), a play modeled on George Bernard Shaw's *Pygmalion.* In the play a young woman, appropriately named Alice Babel, is promised riches and fame if she will abandon ASL and learn one of the artificial manual English systems, or to use Charles Krauel's description, if she will learn "all those IS kind of signs." She is taken under the wing of a Henry Higgins–type character who tutors her in the "better" way of signing. In her new world, she encounters language experiments, all using different forms of signing and manual activity—a virtual Tower of Babel. After learning her lessons, like Eliza in *Pygmalion,* she is taken to a ball, where she performs perfectly. But later she regrets having given up ASL and leaves her tutor.

The play was well received as a timely comment on a new situation. The audience could think about how things had changed: from the old days, when "the sign language" was all the terminology that was necessary, to today, with its dizzying array of new labels.

———— • ————

More important than these new labels—and perhaps in some ways even more bewildering to someone who was raised when "the sign language" was "just something we did"—is the new self-consciousness about signed language, the new way of thinking about the language. This new focus has come about along with recent scientific investigations into signed languages that have confirmed what in some sense Deaf people have known all along: that signed languages are human languages with the potential for rich expression.

We first understood this change in the way Deaf people talk about their language while watching "old home movies" that had recently been uncovered after years in storage. Dating from about 1940 to 1964, these are surprisingly good records of a variety of social activities of the Los Angeles Club for the Deaf (an edited version of this collection appears in *The LACD Story,* 1985), an organization that first provided a haven for newly arrived Deaf people during the war years and later remained an active social center for the community. We recognized typical club scenes, crowds milling about in the clubroom, sitting around the bar, playing group games at picnics, women in beauty contests, and, of course, popular entertainment: performances, songs, skits, and lectures.

The mainstay of club festivities was the signed performance. In one scene from the 1940s we saw a young man signing a song that seemed to be about a young woman, her hair, her ample bust, concluding with a twirl of the body. But this, we were told, was the famous version of "Yankee Doodle" performed by the local favorite, Elmer Priester. We could see the crowds dancing around Priester and sometimes signing along with him, but it seemed to matter less whether everyone was in unison than that they were all joining in as part of a loud, joyous group.

We were reminded of today's Deaf performers, the poets and storytellers of our generation, and the kind of pleasure they bring to an audience, but it was also clear that since 1940 signed performance had changed. It was not simply that we had not recognized "Yankee Doodle."

The most significant difference is the one we have already mentioned: today's performers are much more self-conscious, what we would call analytical, about their language. A modern signed performance may focus on the elements of signed language; in this way, the language itself may be both the medium and the subject of the performance.

A good example of this is a "game" from *My Third Eye* (1973). Until the first performance of this play, all productions by the National Theatre of the Deaf had been signed translations of written works. The first season, for example, featured signed translations of Puccini's *Gianni Schicchi* and poetry by Lewis Carroll and Elizabeth Barrett Browning. It was not until the fourth season, when *My Third Eye* was put together, that members of the company began to experiment with creating their own pieces.

The game appears during a segment called "Manifest," a playful but expertly designed piece in which actors introduce the audience to their language. The game begins when an actor steps out to stage front and announces: "We will show you signs that all have the index finger!" Each actor gives a sign that has the index finger handshape: BLACK, WHO, SCOLD. After completing a round, the cast moves on to another handshape. For the "three" handshape, they demonstrate LOUSY, ELEGANT, and ROOSTER (figure 5.1).

The actors display yet another handshape, the index and middle fingers in a vee—VISIT, STUPID, STUCK—and the game continues. The game is fun to watch, although it tells no story and has no particular dramatic impact apart from its animated listing of signs that share some similarities. The objective of the game is simply to demonstrate a characteristic of signs: that they are made up of smaller parts, including the handshape, its location, its movement, and the orientation of the hand with respect to the body.

In creating this segment, the members of the NTD company discovered a new way of thinking about signs. The actors first look at the audience but then slowly, by changing the direction of their gaze, invite the audience to watch their hands instead of their bodies. As the actors move around the stage, forming new groups for each demonstration, the focus of the performance is on the signs themselves.

———— • ————

If we compare *My Third Eye* and other modern works with filmed records of older performances, such as those found in the LACD collection and in Charles Krauel's collection of old home movies of activities of the National Fraternal Society of the Deaf (the Frat), we can see how much both sytle and content have changed over the years.

One interesting observation about the older films is how little they concentrate on recording signing. As Ted Supalla, the producer of the film about Krauel, explains, Krauel saw himself as a documentarist whose responsibility was to record events for those who were not fortunate enough to attend. He enjoyed showing his films at the club as a kind of local newsreel, narrowly aimed at

Figure 5.1

LOUSY   ELEGANT   ROOSTER

the interests of his community. He thought it important to note for the future the names of hotels where national Frat conventions were held. He made careful film records of the hotel, including shots of the marquee and the building itself. He took shots of the city and the scenery. But he paid little attention to the detail of signing. He did make good records of signed performances, but he devoted relatively little footage to casual signed conversations. Often only short snatches of signed sentences can be seen as his camera pans over groups of people.

In these films, signing is for commentary, to explain where events are taking place, to record names of friends, buildings and parks, or to orient the viewer to the film's content. Krauel did not choose to devote footage to recording signs or describing them. His films do include signed explanations: a friend introduces a couple celebrating their fiftieth wedding anniversary, a woodworking teacher proudly tells about the detailed airplane models his student has made. In the LACD film collection, too, signing is used to headline, explain, demonstrate, and guide. One scene in an LACD film features an animated advertisement for the club by the president: "Our policy is a good time. You'll never feel depressed or down around here!"

In *My Third Eye,* the actors began thinking about signing not as explanation but as object. In their self-conscious performances, they took their language out of the flow of everyday life and made it into an object for theater. Going one step further, they not only extracted the sign from the narrative flow but began to analyze its internal structure, and used the analysis to guide the game.

Priester, in contrast, cared about signing "Yankee Doodle" with patriotism and good cheer. He was not rigid in his sign selections; in fact he apparently took great liberties with his translation. His friends remembered his adult versions of the song, in which he used phallic substitutions for references to cannons. Unfortunately for us today, the filmmakers exercised their good judgment and we have only tasteful performances on record, but we know there was a lot of playfulness and creativity with the language. This intuitive creativity we do not dispute. What we could not find in any of the old films we watched was the focused, analytical sense of the language as object that we see in *My Third Eye*.

Along with "Yankee Doodle," the LACD and Krauel films include many signed performances of a certain type of popular song. This type of song was apparently widely performed in several parts of the United States, but its origin is unclear. In one version filmed by Krauel, a leader stands in front of a group, next to a large board with a list of animals. He leads the group through the list as they sign the song together in a simple rhythm. The trick is to stay in unison for each beat. After each animal sound, the group repeats the sign DARN three times:

> The birds sing, sing, sing, but I hear them not at all,
> Darn, Darn, Darn
> The cats meow, meow, meow but I hear them not at
>   all,
> Darn, Darn, Darn
> The dogs bark, bark, bark but I hear them not at all,
> Darn, Darn, Darn
> The cows moo, moo, moo but I hear them not at all,
> Darn, Darn, Darn.[1]

The refrain "Darn, Darn, Darn" makes this song similar to another set of songs we found in both collections. In these songs, the repetition is done with a distinctive "one, two, one-two-three" rhythm, into which the performer inserts his own vocabulary.

One of the earliest performers of these songs seems to have been a pep-squad leader at Gallaudet College, George Kannapell, who continued his "one, two, one-two-three" routines after he graduated from college in 1930. Kannapell appears in one of Krauel's films with the following song, probably a narrative about going to a convention or on a group tour:

1. Translated by Ted Supalla.

Boat, Boat, BoatBoatBoat
Drink, Drink, DrinkDrinkDrink
Fun, Fun, FunFunFun
Enjoy, Enjoy, EnjoyEnjoyEnjoy.[2]

In the LACD film collection we found a song created by Odean Rasmussen, or "Rasy" as his friends called him, who was the resident "one, two, one-two-three" singer at the LACD clubhouse:

Really, Really, ReallyReallyReally
Excited, Excited, ExcitedExcitedExcited
Packing, Packing, PackingPackingPacking
Farewell, Farewell, GoodbyeGoodbyeGoodbye
Taking the train, Taking the train (or)
        MaybeMaybeMaybe
Hitchhike, Hitchhike, HitchhikeHitchhikeHitchhike
Hitchhike, Hitchhike . . .[3]

These songs all involve fitting a series of signs into the "one, two, one-two-three" rhythm. They all tell a story in some way, as in Rasy's story about leaving home or Kannapell's about the good times to be had at the convention. And they are all group songs, used to incite a crowd to good cheer and a sense of unity. Today they have all but disappeared. Possibly the only one still widely recited is the fight song of Gallaudet College:

Hail to our mighty bisons!
Snort, Snort, SnortSnortSnort
Spirit! And hail to our Gallaudet flag, the Buff and Blue!
Clap, Clap, ClapClapClap
All our enemies are afraid of our Gallaudet men
Because our Gallaudet men give them . . .

2. Translated by Ted Supalla.
3. Translated by Carol Padden and Tom Humphries.

Damn, Damn! Hell, Hell, Hell!
Clap, Clap, ClapClapClap.[4]

———— • ————

Between the time of the "one, two, one-two-three" songs and the creation of *My Third Eye,* as we have said, a major change took place in the way Deaf performers thought about and used their language. Contributing to this change was the development of new descriptions of signed language. One of the first steps toward this kind of analysis of signed language came from a radical proposal by William C. Stokoe for a new way to describe signs. Stokoe broke with the earlier tradition of describing signs as whole "picture" units. Drawing heavily on the work of structuralists like George Trager and Henry Smith, he suggested that each sign can instead be analyzed as being composed of smaller units: its handshape, its movement, and its location on the body. Signs can be decomposed into smaller parts which are then combined in limited ways, just as a spoken word is composed of a sequence of units called phonemes, arranged in rule-governed structures. Thus signed and spoken languages must be far more similar than previously thought, since, at least from the point of view of their internal analysis, there is no basis for treating them differently (Stokoe 1960).

To illustrate his point, Stokoe then published in 1965 a dictionary of "American sign language" "based on linguistic principles." (Note that this is a slight revision of the traditional label, "the sign language." The fully capitalized American Sign Language would not appear until later.) He organized signs not in the traditional way, according to their English translations or by categories such as "animals" or "food," but according to their handshapes, movements, and locations (Stokoe, Casterline, and Croneberg 1965). The dictionary's most innovative feature was a

4. Translated by Wilt McMillen from a poem by Robert Panara, "The Bison Spirit" (1945).

notation system for representing the handshape of the sign (for which he invented the term "dez"), and its movement and location. The entry for NIGHT reads as follows:

$\overline{B}_D$ B_v ˣ

> (dez held so fingertips are lower than wrist, touches or taps across edge of tab; dez contact at heel of hand or inside of wrist) ɴ *night.*

Many considered this notation a bizarre idea. Stokoe's contention that "the sign language" warranted such extensive analysis created a minor stir among his colleagues and students at Gallaudet College. The campus newspaper, the *Buff and Blue,* dutifully reported Stokoe's various achievements, including grants from the American Council of Learned Societies and the National Science Foundation, but as one Deaf colleague, Gilbert Eastman, recalls, "I did not believe Dr. Stokoe would succeed in his project and I thought [his] two deaf assistants were wasting their time signing before the camera" (1980:19). The Deaf community for the most part still believed, much as Krauel did, that signs were best described in terms of how they "felt" and what "picture" they represented. J. Schuyler Long's standard dictionary, *The Sign Language: A Manual of Signs* (1918), had taken a typical approach:

> NIGHT: Place the hands and arms in position as if about to sign for day but move the hand down and describe a semi-circle below the arm from right to left, thus representing the course of the sun during the period of time from set of sun to its rising.

Stokoe, in contrast, wanted a dictionary of ASL that would, like a dictionary of spoken language, list all possible lexical elements and their "pronunciations." Just as a dictionary of the oral language may include an inventory of the possible vowel and consonant combinations, Stokoe's dictionary listed the closed set of handshapes of ASL, with their locations and movements. As it turned out, Stokoe had gotten an early start on what would prove to be a science of signed language.

———— • ————

Coinciding with and contributing to the emergence of this science was a new generation of poets and performers and their art. The gradual convergence of art and science has had a strong impact on art forms. This can be seen in the performances of the actors of the National Theatre of the Deaf (NTD), as mentioned earlier. With funding from the Department of Health, Education and Welfare, the new NTD was established in 1967 with a mandate to bring to the public a new image of Deaf people. Deaf actors who had worked largely for their community, earning only occasional payments for their performances, were now continuously employed as part of a professional repertory. Faced with the task of creating a unique theater company with its own new productions, the performers turned within themselves and mined the rich resource of their language. As one founding member, Lou Fant, tells it, the task of translating material into signed language provoked serious arguments within the company about which "form" of the sign language should be used for the stage (Fant 1980).

The impact of the new way of thinking about the language can also be seen in the poetry of Dorothy Miles and Clayton Valli. In a preface to one of the poems in her book *Gestures,* Miles explains: "This poem developed from a discussion about the similarity between the signs for SHY, SHAME, and WHORE. When I finished writing it, I found that most of the signs I would use had the same handshape" (1976:37). In 1975, Miles visited Ursula Bellugi and her colleagues at the Salk Institute, who were involved in a scientific exploration of signed language structure. Her interaction with the group inspired her to develop more poetry (Miles 1976).

One of Miles's poems, "Total Communication," is an example of the way the language itself has become the subject of signed performance. In this poem we see some of the unusual devices Miles has developed, including her trademark "double translation," or poetry that works in either a signed or a spoken presentation. The poem is based on a handshape, that of the sign for the first person pronoun "I." The first four lines of "Total Communication" are written in English as follows:

> You and I,
> can we see aye to aye,
> or must your I, and I
> lock horns and struggle till we die?

In the third and fourth lines, Miles arranges the sequence of signs so all handshapes are the same. The sign I normally contacts the chest, but, using poetic license, Miles locates it in second-person space, and the result is YOUR-I. Next she maintains the same handshape and signs I, setting up the two hands to come together in the next sign, LOCK-HORNS. Compare the signs I and LOCK-HORNS (figure 5.2) with the line from the poem, "or must your I, and I / lock horns and struggle till we die?" This use of signs allows Miles to show, metaphorically, two people who come together and clash. The detail of keeping the same handshape across a line is small and subtle, and is characteristic of her poetry.

Elsewhere, instead of maintaining the same handshape, she

Figure 5.2   "or must your I, and I / lock horns . . ."

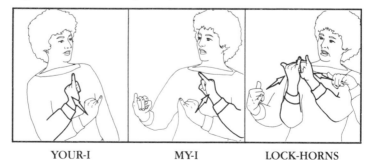

YOUR-I   MY-I   LOCK-HORNS

manipulates the location of signs. In her poem "Defiance," she again uses the sign I in an unfamiliar way:

> If I were I
> I would not say those pleasant things that I say;
> I would not smile and nod my head
> When you say
> No!

Here Miles compares the "real I" and the "hypocritical I." In reference to the second I, the public self, she first signs HYPO-CRITE, and then locates the next sign, I, not on the body as is usual but instead on the handshape of the sign HYPOCRITE— meaning "hypocritical I." The other meaning of I is signed normally, on the body, to represent the "real I," the private self.

The work of another modern poet, Clayton Valli, shows the same awareness of sign structure, as well as manipulation of a different kind. In "Windy Bright Morning" (1985), Valli manipulates not only handshape and location but also the ways the two hands interact:

> Through the open window
> with its shade swinging, sunshine, playful
> taps my sleepy eyes.[5]

Some signs are made with one hand, like the sign I, and some with two hands, like LOCK-HORNS and HYPOCRITE. The beauty of this poem lies in the careful arrangement of one-handed and two-handed signs. Each segment of the poem is deliberately chosen to fit with segments before and after it. In the first line, Valli takes advantage of the fact that the sign WINDOW requires two hands. He sets up the sign WINDOW, then slowly but clearly he moves the hands out of the position for WINDOW and into position for the two one-handed signs WINDOWSILL and CUR-TAIN-EDGE-GENTLY-BLOWING. He simply changes the relation of the hands to each other, flowing into the next two signs

---

5. Translated by Karen Wills and Clayton Valli.

without a break. The result is a very lyrical line with a soft rhythm.

———— • ————

Miles and Valli build their poetry around a detailed awareness of how signs are assembled and the relationship of structure to meaning. Compared to these poets, earlier performers like Priester and Kannapell seem to have taken their language for granted, just as our friend David said his family always had. For Priester, a performance was something one rehearsed and perfected, but not something one planned in the same conscious and careful way we see in the work of Miles and Valli.

But did the earlier performers have any knowledge about the structure of their language? We think so. Priester's adult version of "Yankee Doodle" suggests that he knew at least enough about the language to be able to select signs that subtly suggested another meaning, yet were similar enough to the original song so people would recognize the joke.

Another poem, first performed in 1939, makes it clear that sign performers of past generations did know, intuitively if not explicitly, about the structure of their language. This poem, when it was performed during the NTD's first season, stunned the audience, delighted the critics, and made its performer a national favorite. It is Eric Malzkuhn's translation of Lewis Carroll's "Jabberwocky."

Malzkuhn had first worked on the translation for a poetry contest while a student at Gallaudet College in 1939, and had taken the mixed reaction as evidence that he was attempting something new. He continued to perform the poem at various clubs, always changing the performance slightly according to his whim and the special characteristics of the club. For a Detroit Deaf club, for example, he turned the monsters in the poem into cars of varying sizes and features.

In 1967 Malzkuhn joined the NTD as a coach, and his translation was assigned to a young actor, Joe Velez. Velez, with his lean and lithe style, imparted a new dimension to the performance, and became so well known for his "Jabberwocky" that today his name is inseparably linked to the poem. (Velez's performance can be seen in the film *Tyger, Tyger,* 1967.)

The art of the translation lies in the way Malzkuhn mirrors Carroll's word creations with equally fantastic sign creations. Just as Carroll formed words from parts of other words—"slithy," for example, from "slimy" and "lithe"—Malzkuhn recombined parts of ordinary signs. For the JubJub bird (figure 5.3), he first took parts of signs used for long, thin objects and combined them into one handshape, which he placed on top of the head, to characterize the bird's plumage. Next he recombined the parts of the sign WING to suggest an outlandish creature with double wings on each side of the body. All the other animals in the poem, including the Bandersnatch and the Jabberwock itself, he constructed by playing with various possible combinations of parts of signs such as JAW, MOUND, EYE, FANGS, and TEETH.

For other phrases in the poem, Malzkuhn again used combinations of signs. The sequence "gyre and gimble" involved using a part of a sign for flat surface, but combined with odd movements, suggesting an irregular and spooky wave. For "whiffling through the wood" (figure 5.4), Malzkuhn took parts of signs for broad-footed animals and combined them to form the legs, feet, and flaring eyes of a terrible animal thrashing its way through the brush.

Malzkuhn says he translated the poem strictly by "how it felt."

Figure 5.3 "Jub-Jub bird"

| BIRD | BEAK-LIKE | PLUMAGE |

But, as Ted Supalla first observed (1978), Malzkuhn had stumbled across a central structural property of ASL: the way its morphology, or word-forming system, works.

In spoken languages each word is made up of at least one minimal unit of meaning, called a "morpheme." For example, in English the word "stick" has one morpheme, "stickpin" has two, and "stickpins" has three: "stick," "pin," and the plural "-s."

In his translation, Malzkuhn made clever use of the morphology of his language. To form his sign for "Jabberwock" he combined the morpheme TOOTH with the morphemes HUMP and JAW, resulting in a new combination used as the name for the creature. He exploited the combinative powers of the morphology to create new forms.

But he certainly would not have called his translation an experiment in the "morphology of ASL." In 1939, he had scarcely any idea that his language would be called "ASL," let alone that what he was doing was manipulating its morphology. It would not be until a later generation, when signing began to have names and when performers began to write poetry around sign structure, that Deaf people could think in this way.

———— • ————

Another game in *My Third Eye* also plays with the morphology of ASL. The actors have just finished their handshape game, and

Figure 5.4   The Jabberwock whiffling through the wood

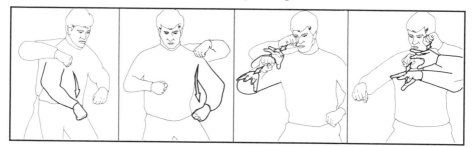

HEAVY-BROAD-FOOTED-TROMPING   EYES-FLARING

one of them, Freda Norman, announces that they will now demonstrate the different ways "we sign brightness." The actors form a line and wait their turns. This time the game is not to think of a sign with some handshape, but to think of a sign sentence that has something to do with brightness.

As the actors present their sentences, they use not the same sign but one of the same two morphemes, either FLASH or SHINE. FLASH is an opening to a spread hand and closing again. SHINE uses the middle finger of an open hand and an outward, wiggling movement. In order to form a sign, these morphemes must then be combined with other parts such as location. Patrick Graybill does BALD-HEAD SHINE, "my bald head shines." Tim Scanlon does SNOW SHINE-HERE SHINE-THERE, "the snow fell and light sparkled on it" (figure 5.5). Richard Kendall shows GUN POLISH-GUN GUN-SHINE, "I polished my gun" (figure 5.6).

Dorothy Miles does one with FLASH: LIGHTHOUSE-ON-HILL FLASH-AND-TURN FLASH-AND-TURN, "the lighthouse flashes in the night." Freda Norman shows PHOTOGRAPH CAMERA-CLICK FLASH, "a flashbulb on a camera went off" (figure 5.7), and Dorothy ends the scene with the delightful BUG FLASH-HERE FLASH-THERE FLASH-THERE CATCH-OBJECT, "I kept seeing a firefly out of the corner of my eye and finally caught it" (figure 5.8).

Here the actors are not only illustrating ASL morphology but have begun to talk about it directly. They understand that the same morpheme, FLASH, appears in both "the lighthouse flashes

Figure 5.5   "Snow fell and light sparkled on it"

SNOW   SHINE   SHINE

Figure 5.6   "I polished my gun"

GUN   POLISH-GUN   GUN-SHINE

in the night" and "the kerosene lamp turns on and off." And the same morpheme that occurs in "my bald head shines" can be found in "the light sparkles on the snow."

If this kind of game were played in English, the actors might take turns thinking of English words containing, say, one of the morphemes "stick" and "sheet." Lipstick. Stickpin. Worksheet. Sheetrock. Pogo stick. Bedsheet. Stick shift. Sheet of steel. Stick of candy. Sheet of paper. Stick of wood. An actor might also try stretching the language to create new images: Sheet of snow on the road. Sheet of water flowing over the wall.

And now we see clearly the difference between Malzkuhn and the actors in *My Third Eye*. In the game, the express purpose of doing the segment is to call the audience's attention to particular properties of the language. The actors use their new understand-

Figure 5.7   "A flashbulb on a camera went off"

PHOTOGRAPH   CAMERA-CLICK   FLASH

ing of the language, that it is made up of smaller units of meaning, as an object for theater. Malzkuhn, in contrast, began with an English poem and built his performance around how to translate it. His translation shows an awareness of the way his language works, but not an analysis of it.

As we have said, the changes we have traced in the style and content of signed performance reflect profound changes in Deaf people's understanding of their language. The performers of the past, like Priester, Kannapell, Rasy, and Malzkuhn, clearly appreciated the creative potential of signed performance, just as their modern counterparts do. What is new is the idea that signs can be thought of—and are well worth thinking of—as objects in themselves.

What the more recent types of performance reveal is not only an emerging science of signed language but a new science of self. Deaf people today have a new self-consciousness about their own culture, including their performances. Where once their signed language and their culture were deeply embedded in larger contexts, they have now been extracted to become objects for analysis.

But it is important to repeat here, as we follow the history of signed performances, songs, and poetry, that Deaf people's deepest knowledge about their signed language has not changed—it has only been confirmed by science and affirmed by artistic ex-

Figure 5.8 "I kept seeing a firefly out of the corner of my eye and finally caught it"

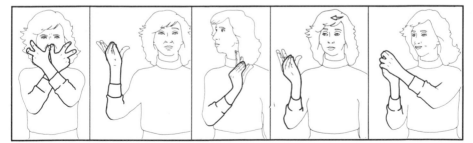

BUG   FLASH-HERE   FLASH-THERE   FLASH-THERE   CATCH-OBJECT

pression. From Veditz's 1913 speech to Malzkuhn's playful "Jabberwocky" to Miles's and Valli's careful, measured poetry, all of the works we have quoted make clear, each in its own way, the rich potential of signed language. It is perhaps polemical to say that the performances of Deaf people showed that they always knew the potential of the language, but they did, after all, know. What we now see is a new reflectiveness about their language and a new vocabulary for describing it.

6

The Meaning of Sound

A widespread misconception among hearing people is that Deaf people live in a world without sound. In *And Your Name Is Jonah* (1979), a network film about a young boy whose parents at first do not realize he is deaf, the boy's perspective is represented in certain scenes by the complete absence of any soundtrack. In one such scene Jonah is taken to a party, and the abrupt shift to an eerie silence, without human voices, other noises, or even background music, conveys to the hearing audience a horrifying sense of isolation and disorientation. Instead of giving the boy's perspective, the scene most likely terrifies the hearing audience into recognizing their own fear of any loss of sound.

That the metaphor of silence is a pervasive one can be seen in titles of books about Deaf people, such as *They Grow in Silence* (Mindel and Vernon 1971), *Dancing without Music* (Benderly 1980), *Growing Old in Silence* (Becker 1980), *The Other Side of Silence* (Neisser 1983). Even Deaf people are sufficiently impressed by the metaphor that they too use it, for example in the titles of their national publications, the *Silent Worker* and the only Deaf-owned newspaper now in circulation, the *Silent News*. Names of Deaf organizations also indicate that Deaf people find this image a useful form of self-reference: the Pacific Silent Club, the Silent Oriole Club, the Chicago Silent Dramatic Club, the Des Moines Silent Club.

To hearing people the metaphor of silence portrays what they believe to be the dark side of Deaf people, not only an inability to use sound for human communication, but a failure to know the world directly. For hearing people, the world becomes known through sound. Sound is a comfortable and familiar means of orienting oneself to the world. And its loss disrupts the way the world can be known. These images communicate the belief that Deaf people cannot have access to the world because it is primarily conveyed by sound and especially by the spoken word. Instead they are locked "on the other side," behind "sound barriers," and are condemned to a life lacking the depth of meaning that sound makes available to hearing people.

There are two ways to think about sound. The most familiar is that sound is a change in the physical world that can be detected by the auditory system. This is the supposedly bare "acoustic" definition. But what is often overlooked is that sound is also an organization of meaning around a variation in the physical world. The classic example of how to distinguish between a wink and an involuntary reaction of the eye, a tic (Ryle 1949, Geertz 1973) can be applied to sound as well. A wink differs from an involuntary closing of the eye not by any difference in the physical process of closing the eye, but by the way it is organized with respect to other activities: a wink is an act of signification, a communication of social meaning to another person. Comparably, the sound of a cough may be a spontaneous by-product of the clearing of the windpipe, or it may be a way to indicate disapproval, or to give a signal.

The fact that different cultures organize sound in different ways shows that sound does not have an inherent meaning but can be given a myriad of interpretations and selections. For example, the phonemic clicks or ingressive stops in Bantu languages may seem like meaningless noise to speakers of English. The widely varying representations for sounds such as a dog's bark ("bow-wow" in English but "oua-oua" in French) make it clear that languages code noises in different ways. There are cultural conventions for what kinds of sound patterns should be used for doorbells, fire alarms, and sirens. And with respect to music, what is spiritually fulfilling for one culture may be bizarre and dissonant to another. The new tradition of American avant-garde music is thrilling to some but confuses people in other cultures. In any discussion of Deaf people's knowledge of sound, it is important to keep in mind that perception of sound is not automatic or straightforward, but is shaped through learned, culturally defined practices. It is as important to know the specific and special meaning of a given sound as it is to hear sound.

An elderly Deaf woman once told us that she had only recently learned that hearing people could hear their own voices. She knew they could hear each other and that they communicated by sound, but somehow, in her ideas about what they were able to do, it had never penetrated that they could actually hear their own voices. This reminded us of another occasion, when we had been helping a friend move her furniture into her parents' house. Her hearing father, a physician, was also helping with the move. At one point, when Tom was wrestling with a difficult piece of furniture, the father tried several times to call out his name. It was not until his daughter reminded him that Tom would not be likely to hear him that he finally realized he could not simply call out by voice to get Tom's attention. Our elderly friend knew that hearing people "hear," and the physician knew that Deaf people "are deaf," but each of them had incomplete theories about the other. Deaf people's theories about sound and how hearing people hear may be imperfect, but no more imperfect than the theories of those who must guess about what it is like to not hear.

———— • ————

When hearing people identify Deaf people as silent, they are mistakenly assuming that Deaf people have no concept of sound, that sound plays no part in their world, or that if it does, their ideas about it are deeply distorted. The truth is that many Deaf people know a great deal about sound, and that sound itself—not just its absence—plays a central role in their lives.

We have heard many reminiscences about the ways Deaf children learn about sound and try to discover its connections to the world. One friend told us about the kinds of activities he and his schoolmates engaged in during his early years at a school for the deaf. The boys' favorite after-school activity was watching a popular film serial of the time called *Blackhawk,* which came with a sound track conveniently concentrated in the bass range. (For many deaf people, the lower frequencies are the most easily detectable, creating not only loud sounds they can hear but vibrations on the floor and furniture.) After each episode, the boys would gather in small groups with their favorite leaders, who would recreate each scene again in the finest detail. By reenacting the episode, the boys could remake the material into their own, taking ownership of what belonged to others. As our friend told us:

> There were some popular ways of doing the stories. We'd start with the beginning of the film. We'd put our hands together, then slowly draw them apart, each hand representing the fabric as the curtains were drawn apart, all the while doing our vocal roars in imitation of the overture. Then we'd do the rolling up of the titles and credits. One boy was my favorite, and everyone else's too. He could transform each episode into a wonderful story with the kind of detail we liked. His aviator scenes were the best, complete with scenes of the pilot barking commands into his radio, his body moving to the side as the airplane banked into a deep dive. Then he'd begin the love scenes with the aviator and his current love interest, mouthing the dialogue just as it was in the film. First the pilot, looking down, would begin to talk in a gruff manner to the woman, then the woman would mouth in response. There were never any real words, simply because he had no idea what was being said between them. But of course, we didn't either.
>
> I remember how he'd do the planes taking off from the runway. He would recreate the sound of the roar during takeoff by putting one arm under his chin, and with the hand cupped around the ear, he would take his other hand, form the sign for airplane-type objects, place it on his arm.

Then he would move his hand down his arm (as if down a runway) and up into the space beyond his arm (takeoff into the air) while roaring his imitation of the sounds of planes. With his hand cupped around his ear, he could hear his own roaring. He was the best.

Other friends told about acting out airplane battles in the hallways, using their hands to represent the airplanes and the walls as runways. Sometimes they would play alone, other times with friends using their airplane-like signs as enemy aircraft. Hallways were favorite places because the reverberation of the children's roars against the narrow halls would make them sound even more like airplanes.

This kind of game as played by Deaf children was showcased in a segment of *My Third Eye.* Like boys who used their hands for airplanes in aerial combat, the actors created a story about a storm at sea, a shipwreck, and a rescue by helicopter. One actor combines handshapes to show a helicopter flying above choppy waves, lowering a rescue chair on the end of a line, and the shipwrecked person gratefully boarding the chair and being lifted into the helicopter, which then flies off to a safe haven. The story unfolds solely through signs, their movements and handshapes, as the ensemble of actors moves in rhythmic unity. The actors, however, in deference to their hearing audiences, refrain from including the roaring soundtrack that real children would be very likely to include.

Another friend told us how he and his young playmates, six to eight years of age at the time, would go into the playroom in the boys' dormitory and invent games that used sound at as loud a volume as they could manage. One game involved a contest to see who could make the loudest sound. "Loud," to them, meant sounds that favored the lower frequencies. The boys learned somewhere, our friend could not remember when or where, that they could make sound louder by projecting it into a corner rather than into the center of the room. They could use the walls as a resonating chamber. And to better direct the sound and increase its volume, they would cup their hands together and direct the voice through the narrow channel of their hands into the corner. Usually the largest boy turned out to be the best at this game. In the confines of their playroom and with their limitless imaginations, the boys began to learn much about the properties of sound.

On other days, these boys would tire of whooping into the corners of the playroom and instead would sit on small chairs and in unison sing-song a particular word—one was "to-mor-row"—over and over again, learning the different ways to make spoken sounds. In another fortuitous discovery, they found that rapping on the windowpanes created deliciously loud noises. They tried as many different variations of these raucous experiments as they could, until at last the hearing counselors could no longer tolerate the whoops, shrieks, blood-curdling yells, pounding of walls, and rattling of windows, and would storm into the room, yelling "You're all nothing but animals!"

These activities were not unique to this one school; other friends recalled having played similar games: whooping into walls, pounding on floors and windowpanes, and using the hallways for launching loud aircraft. All this seemed to be part of the tradition passed down from one generation of schoolchildren to the next, across schools many miles apart.

These stories, just as they vividly paint the inventiveness of childhood, also tell us something about how much young Deaf children must have learned about activities involving sound. From the boys' many experiments, they acquired a great deal of common knowledge about how sound works, how volume and resonance interact in the carrying of sound waves across distances.

———— • ————

Inevitably, at some point in the development of their knowledge about sound, Deaf children begin to understand that one important thing to learn about sound is how hearing people think about it. When our friend told us about the experiments in the playroom, the whooping and shrieking into the walls, he could not remember it without mentioning the hearing counselors' reaction: "You're all nothing but animals!"

A reminiscence by Bernard Bragg in *Deaf Heritage* is a good example of how Deaf children discover very quickly that sound can be a very serious matter:

> Spontaneous outbursts of laughter in the classroom were often stilled by scornful reprimands from our fifth-grade teacher not so much because they were impolite or erupted at inappropriate times as because he said they sounded disgustingly unpleasant or irritating—even animalistic. Young and uncomprehending as we were, we were given long lectures on the importance of being consistently aware of what our laughter sounded like to those who could hear. From that time on, we were forced to undergo various exercises like breathing through the nose only—breathing through the mouth only—either with sound or without— doing these repeatedly with our hands on our stomachs or heads. Compliments were often lavished upon those who came up with forced but perfectly controlled laughter—and glares were given to those who failed to laugh "properly" or didn't sound like a "normal" person . . . Some of us have since then forgotten how to laugh the way we had been taught. And there are two or three from our group, who have chosen to laugh silently for the rest of their lives. (Gannon 1981:355)

Knowing about sound involves not only discovering its acoustic properties but also, and more important, learning the complicated conditions attached to it. Once at a party that had continued late into the night, a small group of us began telling stories about growing up. In the safe intimacy of the group, each new story was more personal than the last. Seizing this rare opportunity, a friend announced that he had a tremendous debt to his older brother. We looked at him, waiting. His brother, he slowly began, had taught him a most valuable lesson: how to urinate in a toilet properly!

The group broke out in laughter, and our friend knew he could continue. His brother had explained to him that, as a deaf child, he should be extremely careful about how he urinated. The sound generated by a certain placement of the stream was very disturbing. He should always aim for the porcelain, *not* into what he had thought to be the logical receptacle, the water. If he neglected this responsibility, people would become very angry with him and think terrible thoughts about him. He reenacted for us his innocent, wide-eyed reaction. He had had no idea that such sounds could be offensive and was horrified at the thought that by the simple act of relieving himself he could incur such disapproval.

We laughed until we were weak. We all knew the little wide-eyed boy he portrayed. He was each one of us. All of us, in our own painful ways, had made similar discoveries, when what we thought was reasonable turned out to have potentially disastrous repercussions.

A woman reflected that it wasn't that we didn't know these things made sounds, but that we didn't know how the sounds would be interpreted. We all nodded enthusiastically. And then she told her story. After four years in a school for the deaf, she had transferred to a public school where she was the only Deaf child. On one fateful day, during a quiet class discussion, she had a terrible bout of flatulence. She silently debated with herself, uncertain about whether releasing gas was like coughing or sneezing. If the urge was equally pressing and involved some bodily function, she reasoned, then it must be equivalent. It would make a noise, she knew, but she didn't think the others would mind. She made her decision. Moments later she discovered to her horror that she had guessed wrong: flatulence is not the same as coughing or sneezing.

Others had stories about digestive noises, which are notoriously troublesome to evaluate. A college student discovered one day in a cafeteria line that an unrestrained belch led the hearing people around him to draw conclusions about his socioeconomic class. And we agreed we were unclear about which kinds of stomach rumblings were detectable. Some noises were more likely to attract glances, but we couldn't seem to predict which ones. And of course, reactions are not always reliable measures. Some stomach rumblings seemed to us to be loud enough to attract attention, while some others did not, perhaps because such noises are so common that people agree not to notice. Or were we being silently condemned? What reactions could we trust? We all had stories about how in restaurants we had to restrain the urge to sip too efficiently from straws, chew as thoroughly as we wanted to, or clear our windpipes after a drink. Many times what we thought were innocent or reasonable sounds turned out to have different significance from what we had thought.

The trick for Deaf people living among hearing people is to figure out the complicated meanings attached to various sounds. Sometimes Deaf people develop good theories about these sounds, but at other times the meanings of sound are much more elusive.

A friend once told us she couldn't figure out what was permissible when she used a public toilet. She reasoned that at least some sounds must be permitted, since it would be impossible to carry out one's functions in complete silence. The problem was, one couldn't simply ask in a bathroom, or even ask a good friend, "Excuse me, but I wonder . . . when you sit down on a toilet, do you . . ." Her humorous portrait of a well-intentioned scholarly type making inquiries into the ways of the natives captured perfectly her bewilderment. One just had to make a reasonable guess and hope to get away with it. She became so worried over this uncertainty that she chose what she decided was the safest route: perform nothing that could result in a sound. But of course this solution did not work. She had become so obsessed with being silent that she could no longer use a public bathroom. Then, one day, she came to her senses and decided she would no longer worry about this. She'd simply do whatever she wanted (within reason, of course), noise be damned! We cheered.

In the comfortable context of a group of friends, we could

laugh at how strangely hearing people think about sound and at our own desperate antics in trying to figure out their system. In fact, we laughed as hard as we did because we knew that elsewhere, as Bragg's story made clear, the subject of sound is not a laughing matter.

—————•—————

Deaf people, along with learning about properties of sound and the meanings attached to it, encounter another sobering lesson: the realm of sound very often involves issues of control. It is not surprising that what others use as a central definition of their own lives, sound, should become a powerful tool of control. One of the most interesting stories we found illustrating this was in a colleague's videotape collection. The story is a recollection of the storyteller's first encounter with a dormitory counselor at her residential school. The story begins when the girl hears that she will have a new counselor at school—a woman who has transferred to the job from a women's prison. At this point we smile in anticipation; stories about former prison guards employed as counselors at Deaf schools are legion.

The new counselor turns out to be a huge, humorless woman who maintains her prison-warden mentality, complete with the drab uniform of a warden, a thick leather belt, and a heavy key ring with a whistle, which she will find useless in this new setting. Her treatment of the girls is unduly rough. Each morning, instead of gently waking them, she flashes the ceiling lights of their bedrooms, tears the covers off them, and, for those who linger a bit too long, pulls pillows from under their heads. Worse, she carries her prison-warden role into the shower, where she insists on watching their every move.

After conveying this strong image of malevolence and relentless control, the storyteller proceeds to the point of the story:

> Now there was this one girl this counselor picked on mercilessly. She was one of those types that unconsciously used her voice when she signed. You know, she'd do little squeals

and grunts and other kinds of noises. This counselor couldn't stand her, thought she was mad. She would yell at her to stop, but of course the poor girl couldn't. It was just the way she talked (lots of Deaf people do this, you know the type) . . . Anyway, the counselor made life miserable for her to the point where all she wanted was to run away. We told her she oughtn't, that we'd find a way. Well, we did, we decided we'd get back at her, and we began making plans . . .

We came up with this plan. We'd set out bait. We'd put this poor girl in the bathroom, get her started on her squealing and stuff, and once we got the counselor after her, into the bathroom, we could trap her and put our plan in action . . . We were in the bathroom and we got her to start squealing and making all kinds of noises . . . and exactly according to plan, the counselor came running down the hall after her. We could even feel her coming, the floors shook at every heavy step . . . She came into the room and didn't even bother to look at us, but looked directly at the poor girl, who then panicked and escaped from the bathroom behind us into the sleeping quarters where she'd be protected. The next part of the plan was to force the counselor to go through us to catch the girl . . . She began chasing after her into the large sleeping room, where a group of us were lined up on either side. She came running down, only one thing on her mind—to catch the poor girl . . . Then one of us extended a leg, and the counselor flew through the air and landed on the floor with a heavy thud.

The retaliation is complete, they have tricked the counselor into humiliation. But then the story takes an unexpected turn.

At long last, we had made up for what she had done to us. We cheered and cheered until . . . we realized she wasn't moving. We very carefully approached her. Maybe she had fainted? We came closer. Then she lifted her head and tried talking to us. (What a useless thing to do! Now, this woman never bothered to learn to sign. Here she was trying to talk to us and we couldn't understand her.) She kept mouthing something to us, and we sensed desperation. Finally, she lifted her arm and her hand hung limply on the floor, dangling from her arm. "She broke her arm!" we screamed.

The girls run to get another adult, and the counselor is taken away. Three weeks later she returns to the dormitory, her arm in a cast, and they anxiously wait to see what will happen next.

We waited for her old self, but it was gone. Instead, this was one of the most loving people, she was sweet, affectionate. And the most surprising of all: she loved that girl, the one she had hated so much before. Loved her more than anything. We couldn't figure it out.

The story has just the right ending. The malevolent character has received a suitable punishment, if perhaps a bit too harsh, and the punishment leads to redemption.

Another counselor said this woman told her she had been under the mistaken impression that Deaf children were like prisoners: bad, insane, and mean. Instead she found we were all good people . . . better organized and more intelligent than those prisoners she worked with. After this she respected us and loved us. And I guess we loved her too . . . She threw away her leather belt, her heavy key ring and whistle. She became what she should have been, a mother to us.[1]

Although the counselor exerts oppressive control over the girls, it is not until she mistreats one of them on the grounds of

1. Translated by Carol Padden and Tom Humphries.

unacceptable noises that they decide to strike back. This supposedly informal story is a powerful one, for it shows how Deaf people can imagine regaining, however briefly, ownership of sound.

Deaf people know that sound belongs to hearing people except in the few situations when they are allowed to use it. As Bragg's story and the reminiscences of our friends tell us, they are very often required to be silent if they cannot master the sound well enough. An example of the tensions that rise from this competition for control of sound can be found in what is known popularly as "the motel joke," a classic in the community. Here is one version:[2]

> A Deaf couple check into a motel. They retire early. In the middle of the night, the wife wakes her husband complaining of a headache and asks him to go to the car and get some aspirin from the glove compartment. Groggy with sleep, he struggles to get up, puts on his robe, and goes out of the room to his car. He finds the aspirin, and with the bottle in hand he turns toward the motel. But he cannot remember which room is his. After thinking a moment, he returns to the car, places his hand on the horn, holds it down, and waits. Very quickly the motel rooms light up, all but one. It's his wife's room, of course. He locks up his car and heads toward the room without a light.[3]

The joke is not on the Deaf man who has inconveniently forgotten which room is his, but on hearing people, who conveniently help him to find his room. The joke's hero knows he can count on hearing people to be extraordinarily attentive to sound—to his gain and their detriment. Their predictable behavior, to respond to sound even in the middle of the night, is what makes the joke wickedly funny. The audacity of the hero,

---

2. For additional discussion of jokes in the Deaf community, see Rutherford (1983).

3. Translated by Carol Padden and Tom Humphries.

having the nerve to prey upon the automatic instincts of hearing people, is for a moment, thrilling.

Because hearing people's ownership of sound goes almost unchallenged, the joke and the stories create relief of an important kind. The joke turns the tables on hearing people and creates a world where sound can be used to Deaf people's advantage. In a good story, a Deaf storyteller can expertly arrange a sequence of events that allow Deaf people a glimpse of a world where others can be made to repent for their unreasonable ideas.

———•———

There is yet another way in which the metaphor of silence is inadequate. Various cultures of hearing people organize sound in layers of meaning that represent concepts they call "harmony," "variation," "resonance," and "dissonance." As signified by the many film and television portrayals of Deaf people longing to hear the sound of a guitar or piano, many hearing people assume that because Deaf people cannot hear music they cannot appreciate such concepts. Thinking of Deaf people as silent makes it impossible to recognize that, in certain aspects of their lives, they find ways to represent such concepts.

To illustrate this point, we draw from a collection of poems that manipulate the movement of signs not only to convey grammatical content but to impart a subtle impression of rhythmic quality. Clayton Valli's simple ASL poem "Windy, Bright Morning" is one such example. When we first saw it performed in Boston in 1980 we were struck by the power of its rhythmic images, which are created not by the individual signs but by the clever organization of movement within and between signs.

The poem describes the edge of wakefulness and sleep and begins with a window and an external force:

Through the open window
with its shade swinging, sunshine, playful,
taps my sleepy eyes.

The hand, used to represent the shade, moves in a slightly irregular but not unpleasant rhythm.

> Breezes dance in my room,
> around me, not shy, but gentle,
> letting me know that it's time
> to get up! Slowly I wake,
> my eyes stung by sunlight
> flashing past the swinging shade
> that seems to know I'm deaf.

The presence of the light is unmistakable; the movement revolves around the center of the light.

> I stand up, tired, ignoring the light,
> chilled in the dancing air
> that meets me by the window
> I closely shut it. And with the shade still,
> my room darkens.

The irregular movement abruptly ceases, and the room becomes silent. As Valli moves back to the familiar bed, movement is slow and comforting.

> Happy
> back under the covers,
> I'm drowsy, purring, warm . . .

The audience, lulled by Valli's slow delivery, is unprepared for the next verse:

> But suddenly, how strange!
> The shade flaps wildly,
> bright, dark, bright, dark, bright
> Fierce wind flung open the window . . .
> so bitter cold, so cold, the wind, the shade,
> the storm!

The movement is wild and unpredictable. Valli as experiencer widens his eyes and moves his body with a sense of urgency.

Slowly I rise, and try to make them calm down.

As he moves toward the window, the movement, formerly dissonant, changes again, beginning to come together in one organized and focused form:

> The wind, the shade, dancing gracefully, happy.
> One bright ray gently pulls me
> to raise up the shade
> like unwrapping a gift.
> Warm sunlight tickles me,
> morning breeze laughs with me . . .
> Joyful, I welcome the day.[4]

Valli's variations take the form of varying movement within the sign, first sunshine that taps then stings, then the more forceful flapping and startling contrasts of brightness and darkness. We watch Valli arrange signs so they flow one into the next, a soft repeating rhythm, and then the irregular staccato of the flapping. He brings the shades together, then sharply pulls them apart. The closing verse has yet another kind of rhythm, an expansive softness, glowing and enveloping, "like unwrapping a gift." The lingering feeling one has long after watching the poem performed is the arrangement of sensation: the harmony and softness in the lines, the chaotic, dissonant elements, and their contrast with the harmonious conclusion.

"Eye Music," by Ella Lentz, recreates a familiar experience for many deaf people, watching the rhythm of the everyday world. In this poem the central image is watching telephone wires from inside a moving vehicle. Lentz introduces the title by first using the fingers to represent telephone wires, then repositioning them to represent lines on a music sheet, then turning them back into telephone wires that move up and down. This is what she calls "eye music."

---

4. Translated by Karen Wills and Clayton Valli.

The eye music of the telephone wires
with the music sheets
with the lines that rise and quiver,
    sway and lower
along with the passing of space and time . . .

Interspersed with the wires that move up and down horizontally are staccato poles arranged vertically. A telephone pole passing by followed by two in rapid succession has the same effect as a drum with a one, one-two beat (see figure 6.1).

Eyes are the ears
    and the piano and flute are the wires
    and the occasional pole is the drum!

Figure 6.1   "and the occasional pole is the drum"

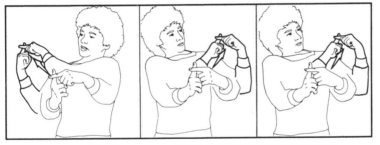

A-POLE-GOES-BY   TWO-POLES-GO-BY-QUICKLY

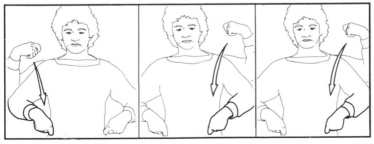

DRUM-BEAT   TWO-QUICK-DRUMBEATS

Then the rhythm of the telephone lines is preserved while Lentz changes the handshape to indicate the number of horizontal lines in the rhythm, from one to five:

> Here is one bold wandering wire and
> Now! here are five dancing . . .
>   high and low in turns
>   with the rhythm of the poles.
> Five disappearing into one again
> And then a crowd,
> overlapping . . . quickly and then slowly . . .
> So beautiful to the eye and heart,
>   one wonders what happens inside . . .[5]

Like Valli, Lentz plays with variations in the rhythm, soft and flowing, fast and rapid, jerking up and down, large and steady. Both poems involve some outside source—sunlight and wind, telephone wires speeding past—that disrupts some ongoing rhythm in a distinctive way. And the poets as experiencers react either in synchrony with or in opposition to the movement of the hands.

In these poems, the organization of movement in signs and the organization of the body in relation to the hands seem to be, to use the language of others, noisy rather than silent. The contrast and coordination of the different components of movement, such as the movement of the hands with that of other parts of the body, create, again using the language of others, a form of counterpoint.

These poems show how movement, as well as sound, can express notions like harmony, dissonance, resonance. We are not suggesting that these movements are replacements for sound or even analogous to sound, for as we have demonstrated, sound itself is not absent from Deaf people's lives but is an integral part of the way they organize experience. Instead, these poems show how Deaf people's own resources, notably movement and the

5. Translated by Ella Lentz.

potential of their language, can be mined to create rich layers of meaning beyond the simply denotative to the realm hearing people assign to music.

————— • —————

Deaf people construct their world around the resources of movement, form, *and* sound. The metaphor of silence has explanatory power for hearing people, emphasizing as it does what they believe to be the central fact about Deaf people. However, it is clumsy and inadequate as a way of explaining what Deaf people know and do. The lives of Deaf people are far from silent but very loudly click, buzz, swish, pop, roar, and whir.

7

Historically Created Lives

Our approach in this book has been to shift attention away from deafness itself to the way Deaf people live—to their culture. We have taken this approach in order to introduce a new way of thinking about what it is to be Deaf. But this does not mean we are ignoring the fact that Deaf people do not hear or that we are treating it as unimportant. Indeed, our point is that the biological characteristic of not hearing is intimately bound up with Deaf people's culture and language. Deafness is a given, a fundamental aspect of their world. This is what we mean when we say we want to look at their lives from "a different center."

Many of the stories we have recounted are about what Deaf people consider to be "possible" and "not possible" lives for themselves. While deafness may not be talked about directly in some of these stories, it is always understood, always central. For example, in Chapter 2 we described a scene from *My Third Eye* in which the actors conjure up a frightening image of a young woman drowning because others insist that she must use speech. In this scene the actors dramatize a collective intuition about what kind of life is *not* possible for Deaf people: a speaking life that excludes signed language. The desperation of the woman at the hands of her tormentors mirrors the deep fear of Deaf people that they may be forced to use a language intended for people with different biological characteristics.

This theme of battling against lives proposed by others is one that has endured through many generations. In the same 1913 film series that features George Veditz (see Chapter 2), Robert McGregor tells a story that rebukes others' beliefs about what kinds of lives are possible for Deaf people. He begins by citing a rude ethnic joke that was current at the time:

> Ladies and gentlemen, always when I hear about the "restored to society deaf," it reminds me of the story of the Irishman and the flea. The Irishman had this flea that would pester him here, there, and everywhere on his body until finally he could no longer stand it. He stripped off his clothing to get at it and managed to catch it, but as soon as he caught it in his hand, and opened his hand to look at it, it would jump back on his body. He'd have to look for it again, catch it, but as soon as he caught it, and opened his hand to look at it, it would jump back on his body, and so on. He could never catch it. This is exactly how it is when often one hears about some deaf man out in Boston: clever, sophisticated, speaks like the hearing, lipreads faultlessly. We'd say, "Really?" and get on the first train out, arrive and ask "Where is he?" "Oh, must be some mistake, he's out in New York!" "Really?" and then we'd hightail it to New York on a horse. "Well, where is this man? Clever, sophisticated, speaks like the hearing?" "Oh, he's in Chicago!" "Drat!" And we'd get back on the train for Chicago, but of course we'd never find him. Always (like the flea), he'd be here, there, or everywhere. Now, I ask you, will we ever find someone who is just as they say: clever, sophisticated, speaks like the hearing, mingles effortlessly with people? Never![1]

McGregor is mocking the oralist ideal of the "restored to society deaf," a deaf person who has overcome the limitations of his "handicap" and is successfully integrated in the world of others. A "clever and sophisticated" person is one who can discuss those intellectual topics which others consider important.

---

1. Translated by Carol Padden and Tom Humphries.

One who "speaks like the hearing" is to be admired because he can converse easily using others' language. And the ideal deaf person is one who "mingles effortlessly with people" because he avoids the embarrassment of halting and failed communication. The rude joke is an angry response to the oralist program, the longing of others to shape Deaf people into people who do not seem deaf at all.

Deaf people must live almost entirely within the world of others. This peculiar social condition leads to a longing of their own, a longing to live lives designed by themselves rather than those imposed by others.

———— • ————

In the 1850s a brief burst of dialogue erupted over the idea that perhaps Deaf people could shake free of others if they relocated to a settlement of their own. John James Flournoy, a Deaf property owner in Georgia, urged the establishment of a separate Deaf state "out west" (Flournoy 1856:122) because, he claimed, "our peculiar necessities and such arrangements as may be indispensable to our welfare, are not known or provided for" (1858:150). Deaf people needed a separate commonwealth, "a political independence, a state sovereignty" (1858:142).

The proposal provoked a spirited debate, much of which appeared in letters to the editor of the *American Annals of the Deaf and Dumb* (1856–1858). Most Deaf leaders ridiculed Flournoy— what did he propose Deaf residents should do with hearing children or hearing siblings? Prohibit them from owning land in the state? And how did Flournoy propose to collect enough revenue to support the state? Shortly after the initial flurry of letters, the plan was abandoned. But even those who considered Flournoy's scheme preposterous were willing to discuss the premise of a settlement of some kind. Edmund Booth, for example, one of Flournoy's main opponents in the debate, conceded that he too had contemplated founding a community of Deaf people:

[the] idea of having a community of deaf-mutes is to me nothing new. In the year 1831, William Willard and five or six others, including myself, formed ourselves into an association with a view of purchasing land in some favorable spot in the west, and so arranging that we might, through life, live in close neighborhood . . . One of our objects had been to form a nucleus around and within which others of our class might, in process of time, gather.   (1858:72–73)

Booth recognized Deaf people's need to be not only one another's friends but one another's neighbors, to create together not only a culture but a society. The editor of the *Annals,* Edward Allen Fay, had a similar idea: "The most feasible of all, in our opinion, would be for two or three or more deaf-mutes, having the money and the capacity for such an undertaking, to select themselves and purchase a few thousand acres of land, and sell it out at a low rate to such deaf-mutes, with their friends, as would become actual settlers" (1858:140). Like Booth, Fay saw the need for at least a town of some kind where Deaf people could live within a group larger than the family—a neighborhood of Deaf people.

Flournoy gained almost no support for complete separatism, and since his time there have been no proposals for a Deaf state, although there have been many calls for political self-determination on a smaller scale.[2] His proposal received little sympathy not only because it was extreme but probably also because he was seen as eccentric and "of unbalanced mind" (Fay 1884).

But what is most interesting about Flournoy's bold proposal is his insistence that Deaf people are bound together by certain needs so compelling, so crucial, that they can be met only through a strong political realization such as a state. Flournoy's phrase "peculiar necessities" calls to mind Clifford Geertz's characterization of ethnic groups as bound together by what he calls "primordial attachments." Their shared characteristics derive not

2. For additional discussion see Winzer (1986), Crouch (1986, 1987), Coulter (1942).

from social interaction but from "a sense of natural—some would say spiritual—affinity" (1973:259–260). Unlike groups that simply share a class, a profession, or some other casual interest, ethnic groups share a more fundamental human feature such as a religion or a language. Ethnic groups often agitate for statehood or some other kind of political self-determination. Even if Deaf people in Flournoy's time were not willing to form a state, the fact that they proposed settlements of some kind shows that they had sentiments much like those of other ethnic groups.

———•———

Two anecdotes from friends of ours hint at what Deaf people's "peculiar needs" are. As part of his teaching internship, our friend Jerry was assigned to teach reading and writing to a small class of deaf students in an inner-city public junior high school. Because these were "mainstreamed" students, not students in a traditional residential program, he expected to find that some had not seen very many other deaf people, or even a Deaf adult. Jerry himself had attended such a school when he was younger, but after a few years had joined his older brother at a residential school for deaf children. He could remember feeling, at the public school, that his social world seemed small. He wanted to feel he could move freely within the school, and from the classroom to a social life outside of school, but he understood that the school belonged to others; he was merely a special student.

But as much as Jerry identified with his new students, he was not prepared for their reaction to him. "I had never seen a group of students so eager to talk with me. All I did was introduce myself, sign with them, and they were instantly attracted to me. They followed me around for days and looked for every excuse to be signing with me." He willingly complied with their demands for more stories and more conversations, but he found their obsessive attraction to him almost alarming.

Another colleague, Sam Supalla, undertook a research project to study sign language development in a small group of young deaf children who had not been exposed to ASL (Supalla 1986).

Although their teachers used an artificial pedagogical sign system and some had hearing parents who also used the system, none had previously been exposed to ASL, among either their classmates or their teachers. Sam recalled that when he first introduced himself to the children by signing to them, he caused a commotion. The children "mobbed" him, each clamoring for his attention. He did not fully understand at the time why they had responded so strongly. It could not be that they saw him as like themselves, another deaf person, for he had earlier discovered that many did not know how to identify a deaf person. One child, for example, claimed his hearing mother was deaf because she signed.

Jerry and Sam were not describing children who were simply excited about new visitors to their classrooms; they portrayed the children as "compelled," "captivated," and "obsessive." These anecdotes remind us of the Abbé de l'Epée's light at the end of a dark road (see Chapter 2): the glimpse of solace in the form of a community of signers.

These anecdotes take place in a distinctly modern setting. Changes in public sentiment about "asylums" or residential schools, and in the economics of education, have brought about a profound change in the way deaf children are educated. Veditz's dark world of oralism, in which educators tried to eliminate signing, has given way to an uncertain world of "mainstreaming," where deaf children face a different kind of isolation.

Public Law 94-142, the Education for All Handicapped Children Act of 1975, declares that deaf children are entitled to an education in their local school districts. The idea of "integrating the handicapped" with the larger population has an inherent attraction, but the mainstreaming movement has caused disruptions in the education of deaf children. One result is that state funding has shifted away from residential schools to supporting school districts; in some states districts are required to pay a charge for each child taken out of the district and sent to a residential school. Within a decade under this law, residential schools that had once enrolled as many as five hundred children found themselves with as few as one hundred and fifty. Enrollment of deaf children in public schools has grown, but because there are so many public schools, any particular school is likely to ˚have only a small number of deaf students. In addition, public schools often find it more economical to adapt existing resources rather than to hire people who have traditionally staffed residential schools. And public schools are not likely to understand the need for a community of Deaf people; public schools with mainstreamed deaf children are often only minimally connected to the surrounding community of Deaf people. The result of these changes is that there are many young deaf children who, although they may be grouped in classrooms with a few other deaf students, have never met a Deaf person and have never seen ASL. As Jerry and Sam's stories tell us, the new social order of "mainstreaming," instead of introducing new worlds to deaf children, may well lead them to a new kind of isolation.

——— • ———

Human children are born with an innate ability to learn language, to create worlds of meaning, but they are also dependent on other language users. The model of human development assumes that each child is born into an environment that provides adult models for learning a natural language. But deaf children born into hearing families often do not have access to such models; they do not hear the spoken English of their parents and neighbors, and they are isolated from Deaf signers.

In 1977 Susan Goldin-Meadow and Heidi Feldman began videotaping a group of profoundly deaf preschool children who were isolated from other signers. Except for limited contact with other deaf children like themselves, they were exposed only to the speaking behaviors of their families. Their parents did not sign, and their schools had policies against the use of signed language in classes (Goldin-Meadow and Feldman 1977).

Despite their isolation from signers and their parents' strong encouragement to use speech, the children began creating first single gestures and then strings of gestures to represent people, objects, and actions. Goldin-Meadow and Feldman were observing modern-day cases similar to what took place in Jean Massieu's family in the 1700s (see Chapter 2). As Massieu explained, he and his deaf siblings developed signs to "express ideas" to one another, but he did not learn the signs of "educated deaf-mutes" until he entered school. And the "home signs" Deaf teachers often observe in newly arrived young deaf pupils, Goldin-Meadow and Feldman identified as invented gestural systems that lack input from a natural language model.

The children Goldin-Meadow and Feldman studied based many of their gestures on bits and pieces of human movement around them, such as pointing gestures and wagging of the hand to show disapproval. But they appropriated other kinds of movement too. Each time Feldman visited one young boy, she would greet him by shaking his hand. Soon the child devised a gesture, shaking the hand, as a "name" for Feldman and used it to represent her to his parents. The same child studied the act of twisting the lid off a jar and used it as a basis for a gesture meaning "jar." The children also used their hands to mimic the sizes and shapes of objects around them, from balls to pencils.

As Mylander and Goldin-Meadow (1986) point out, the children's gestures could not be arbitrary or nonsensical, since it was vital that others understand them. The overt pictorial nature of these gestures—the twisting of a jar, the shape of a ball—allowed adults to join in the child's symbolic world. Goldin-Meadow reports that although parents tried to discourage the use of gestures, many understood them and even used them with their children. These gestures were not simply idle inventions but tools used by the children to participate in the cultural world around them. And for these children gestures were the primary tool of communication, for, as Goldin-Meadow and Mylander (1984b) explain, they developed very little speech and did not use their speech to the same extent as their gestures.

One child, assigned the fictitious name David, was particularly prolific in creating gestures. During the two years of the study, which began when he was two years, ten months old, David created mostly simple sentences with a single proposition, but he also produced approximately 350 more complex two-proposition sentences (Goldin-Meadow 1982). His parents copied some of his gestures and used some combinations with him, but his inventory far exceeded theirs in number of gestures and ability to combine them into sentences.

David's achievement seems remarkable, but in fact, this phenomenon of independent invention among deaf children of hearing families is not rare. A great many deaf children arrive at school with similar repertoires, some more extensive than others.

While it is easy to see how these invented gestures are not like speech, it is important to note that they are also different from natural signed languages. Invented gestural systems lack certain properties found in natural languages, including a range of syntactic structures, such as the passive structure and dative movement (Goldin-Meadow 1982); the gestural systems rely on a simpler syntax. In addition, although David seems to have developed a rudimentary morphological system, certain complex forms found in ASL are absent from his repertoire. Presumably these forms are dependent on input from a model of the language and cannot be invented in isolation (Mylander and Goldin-Meadow 1986).

There is one other crucial difference. Natural signed languages, like spoken languages, have histories; they have been passed down through generations of signers or speakers. But invented gestural systems are created from bits and pieces that are unconnected either to the richer speech of hearing parents or to the richer signed language of Deaf people. What is so fascinating about a case like David's is that it is an example of an attempt to invent a language within one lifetime. The attempt shows that the human need for language is strong, but no individual—not even the Abbé de l'Epée, for all the credit he is given for "inventing" signed language—can hope to match the productivity or complexity of a language constructed over generations of users.

By definition, languages are historically created, not invented by individuals (Clark and Clark 1977).

——— • ———

The inventions of David and other deaf children in hearing families suggest, at the very least, that not hearing must play a role in the kinds of lives deaf people construct for themselves. These inventions would not have been necessary had there been a congruence between the individual's biological construct and the culture. Hearing children born to hearing families do not require special conditions to learn a spoken language, nor do they invent gestures such as these. And deaf children born to Deaf families have no need to invent new forms, because the signed language of their families is sufficient. In both cases, the culture and language of the group, whether hearing or Deaf, have evolved over generations to fit the group's biological characteristics.

Perhaps the greatest risk to deaf children is that they are likely to be born into worlds that do not accommodate their particular biological characteristics. An ongoing social experiment in Sweden shows one way that political resources can be used to overcome the isolation from language of young deaf children born to hearing families. The Swedish government, acting on suggestions from the Deaf community and parents of deaf children, has recently recognized Swedish Sign Language as the nation's official sign language. Parents of deaf children are required to take classes in Swedish Sign Language, and the government sponsors daycare centers where very young deaf children can have Deaf and hearing caretakers who use Swedish Sign Language (Wikstrom 1987). In the United States, there are elementary-level teachers who teach "remedial" ASL to young deaf children whose skill in the language is delayed. They give evidence that, by doing simple exercises analyzing signs and creating sign stories of their own, the children not only develop increased skill in signed language but also become better equipped to approach other kinds of analytical language tasks such as reading (Marbury 1986). Both of these experiments shift the emphasis away from the traditional solutions, teaching of speech and speaking skills, to solutions that use resources of Deaf people—their language and their social practices.

———— • ————

We can imagine a broad range of possible lives for Deaf people, incorporating various communicative strategies. In this book we have portrayed a possible life that involves the use of a signed, not spoken, language. The American example is just one possible solution—there are many others. For example, Italian Deaf people also use a signed language, but they use mouthing and lip-reading more prominently than do American Deaf people. They mouth names of individuals, places, and other borrowed Italian vocabulary, whereas American Deaf people either fingerspell English words or translate them into signs. American Deaf people, according to the Italian counterparts, "barely move their mouths" and "fingerspell rapidly." To represent Danish words, Deaf people in Denmark use a manual system that disambiguates mouthed vowels and consonants. This system is used along with the signed language of the culture. And there must be other types of solutions not yet described. But we believe that what these possible lives will have in common is that they will incorporate the crucial biological characteristics of the individuals that make up the culture, and that they will all be historically created, that is, created over generations of users.

Ways of living proposed for Deaf people that ignore their past, that attempt to remove, either directly or indirectly, their historically created solutions, are not possible lives. A widespread invention, found in communities of people who do not hear throughout the world, is a natural signed language. When deaf children are denied connections with Deaf people, or are prevented from learning a signed language, they lose access to a history of solutions created for them by other people like themselves.

Studying the culture of Deaf people provides an interesting perspective on culture in general and on the relationship between human beings and the properties of their cultures. In nearly all descriptions of the acquisition of language and culture, it is assumed that children have access to adult models of a human language. It is also assumed that children have access to some historically evolved approaches to interpreting the world, to their parents' systems of meaning. And it is assumed that children have access to their parents' collective solutions to common life problems such as how to carry on conversations and how to conduct other kinds of social negotiations. But Deaf people offer a contrast: in many of their lives there are disconnections with the past. The isolation and deprivation experienced by many young deaf children before they discover the language and the culture of Deaf people—and the sense of light after long darkness when they do discover them—allow us to see more clearly the importance of being connected to the past.

Deaf culture is a powerful testimony to both the profound needs and the profound possibilities of human beings. Out of a striving for human language, generations of Deaf signers have fashioned a signed language rich enough to mine for poetry and storytelling. Out of a striving to interpret, to make sense of their world, they have created systems of meaning that explain how they understand their place in the world. That the culture of Deaf people has endured, despite indirect and tenuous lines of transmission and despite generations of changing social conditions, attests to the tenacity of the basic human needs for language and symbol.

References

Index

References

Aissen, J. 1983. "Indirect Object Advancement in Tzotzil." In *Studies in Relational Grammar* I, ed. D. Perlmutter. Chicago: University of Chicago Press.

And Your Name Is Jonah. 1979. A Norman Felton-Stanley Production. Charles Fries Productions and Capital Cities Communication. Video.

Baker, C. 1980. *American Sign Language: A Teacher's Resource Text.* Silver Spring, Md.: TJ Publishers.

Baker, C., and R. Battison, eds. 1980. *Sign Language and the Deaf Community: Essays in Honor of William C. Stokoe.* Silver Spring, Md.: National Association of the Deaf.

Becker, G. 1980. *Growing Old in Silence.* Berkeley: University of California Press.

Bellugi, U., and M. Studdert-Kennedy, eds. 1980. *Signed and Spoken Language: Biological Constraints on Linguistic Form.* Weinheim, German Democratic Republic: Verlag Chemie.

Benderly, B. L. 1980. *Dancing without Music: Deafness in America.* Garden City, N.Y.: Anchor Press/Doubleday.

Bloomfield, L. 1933. *Language.* New York: Holt, Rinehart, and Winston.

Booth, E. 1858. "Mr. Flournoy's Project." *American Annals of the Deaf and Dumb* 10:72–79.

Bragg, B., and E. Bergman. 1981. *Tales from a Clubroom.* Washington, D.C.: Gallaudet College Press.

Burnes, B. 1950. "The Editor's Page." *Silent Worker* 2:2.

Charles Krauel: Profile of a Deaf Filmmaker. 1986. Produced by T. Supalla. Champaign: University of Illinois. Film.

Clark, H., and E. Clark. 1977. *Psychology and Language.* New York: Harcourt Brace Jovanovich.

Collums, C. 1950. "Letter to the Open Forum." *Silent Worker* 2:31.

Coulter, E. M. 1942. *James Jacobus Flournoy: Champion of the Common Man in the Antebellum South.* Savannah: Georgia Historical Society.

Crouch, B. A. 1986a. "Alienation and the Mid-Nineteenth-Century American Deaf Community: A Response." *American Annals of the Deaf* 131:322–324.

———— 1986b. "A Deaf Commonwealth." In *Encyclopedia of Deaf People and Deafness,* ed. J. Van Cleve. New York: McGraw-Hill.

Eastman, G. 1980. "From Student to Professional: A Personal Chronicle of Sign Language." In *Sign Language and the Deaf Community,* ed. C. Baker and R. Battison. Silver Spring, Md.: National Association of the Deaf.

Erting, C. 1985a. "Cultural Conflict in a School for Deaf Children." *Anthropology and Education Quarterly* 16:225–243.

———— 1985b. "Sociocultural Dimensions of Deaf Education: Belief Systems and Communicative Interaction." *Sign Language Studies* 47:111–125.

Fant, L. 1980. "Drama and Poetry in Sign Language: A Personal Reminiscence." In *Sign Language and the Deaf Community,* ed. C. Baker and R. Battison. Silver Spring, Md.: National Association of the Deaf.

Fay, E. A. 1858. "The Plans for a Community of Deaf-mutes." *American Annals of the Deaf and Dumb* 10:136–140.

———— 1884. "Discussion by the National Academy of Sciences Concerning the Formation of a Deaf Variety of the Human Race." *American Annals of the Deaf and Dumb* 29:70–77.

Flournoy, J. J. 1856. "Mr. Flournoy to Mr. Turner." *American Annals of the Deaf and Dumb* 8:120–125.

———— 1858. "Reply to Objections." *American Annals of the Deaf and Dumb* 10:140–151.

Gannon, J. R. 1981. *Deaf Heritage: A Narrative History of Deaf America.* Silver Spring, Md.: National Association of the Deaf.

Geertz, C. 1973. *The Interpretation of Culture.* New York: Basic Books.

Goldin-Meadow, S. 1982. "The Resilience of Recursion: A Study of a Communication System Developed without a Conventional Language Model." *Language Acquisition: The State of the Art,* ed. E. Wanner and L. Gleitman. Cambridge: Cambridge University Press.

Goldin-Meadow, S., and H. Feldman. 1977. "The Development of Language-like Communication without a Language Model." *Science* 197:401–403.

Goldin-Meadow, S., and C. Mylander. 1984a. "The Effects and Non-effects of Parental Input on Early Language Development." *Monograph of the Society of Research in Child Development* 49:1–121.

———— 1984b. "The Nature of Input and Its role in the Development of the Deaf Child's Gesture System." *Monograph of the Society for Research in Child Development,* 49:143–151.

Gustason, G., and J. Woodward. 1973. *Recent Developments in Manual English.* Washington, D.C.: Gallaudet College Press.

Jacobs, L. 1974. *A Deaf Adult Speaks Out.* Washington, D.C.: Gallaudet College Press.

Klima, E., and U. Bellugi, with R. Battison, P. Boyes-Braem, S. Fischer, N. Frishberg, H. Lane, E. Lentz, D. Newkirk, E. Newport, C. Pedersen, and P. Siple. 1979. *The Signs of Language.* Cambridge, Mass.: Harvard University Press.

Kyle, J., and B. Woll, eds. 1983. *Language in Sign: An International Perspective on Sign Language.* London: Croom Helm.

The LACD Story. 1985. Produced by J. DeBee. Distributed by Beyond Sound, Los Angeles. Film.

Lane, H. 1976. *The Wild Boy of Aveyron.* Cambridge, Mass.: Harvard University Press.

———— 1984. *When the Mind Hears: A History of the Deaf.* New York: Random House.

Lane, H., and F. Philip. 1984. *The Deaf Experience: Classics in Language and Education.* Cambridge, Mass.: Harvard University Press.

Lane, H., and F. Grosjean, eds. 1980. *Recent Perspectives on ASL.* Hillsdale, N.J.: Erlbaum.

Lentz, E. 1979. "Eye Music." Produced by the Indiana Committee for the Humanities, Fort Wayne Public Library. Video.

Long, J. 1918. *The Sign Language: A Manual of Signs.* Washington, D.C.: Gallaudet College Press.

McGregor, R. P. 1913. *The Irishman and the Flea.* Silver Spring, Md.: National Association of the Deaf. Film.

Mallery, G. 1972. *Sign Language among North American Indians.* The Hague: Mouton.

Marbury, N. 1986. "ASL and English: A Partnership." Paper presented at the American Sign Language Research and Teaching Conference, Fremont, Calif.

Markowicz, H., and J. Woodward. 1978. "Language and the Maintenance of Ethnic Boundaries in the Deaf Community." *Communication and Cognition* 2:29–38.

Maxwell, M., and S. Smith-Todd. 1986. "Black Sign Language and School Integration in Texas." *Language in Society* 15:81–94.

Miles, D. 1976. *Gestures.* Northridge, Calif.: Joyce Motion Picture Co.

Mindel, E., and M. Vernon. 1971. *They Grow in Silence: The Deaf Child and His Family.* Silver Spring, Md.: National Association of the Deaf.

My Third Eye. 1973. National Theatre of the Deaf. Waterford, Conn. Video.

Myklebust, E. 1957. *Psychology of Deafness.* New York: Grune and Stratton.

Mylander, C., and S. Goldin-Meadow. 1986. "Home Sign Systems in Deaf

Children: The Development of Morphology without a Conventional Language Model." Paper presented at the Conference on Theoretical Issues in Sign Language Research, Rochester, N.Y.

Neisser, A. 1983. *The Other Side of Silence.* New York: Knopf.

Padden, C. 1986. "American Sign Language." In *Encyclopedia of Deaf People and Deafness,* ed. J. Van Cleve. New York: McGraw-Hill.

————— 1988a. "Grammatical Theory and Signed Languages." In *Linguistics: The Cambridge Survey,* ed. F. Newmeyer. Cambridge: Cambridge University Press.

————— 1988b. *The Interaction of Morphology and Syntax in American Sign Language.* Outstanding Dissertations in Linguistics, Series IV. New York: Garland Press.

Panara, R. 1945. "The Bison Spirit." Block "G" Club, Gallaudet College.

Perlmutter, D. 1986. "No Nearer to the Soul." *Natural Language and Linguistic Theory* 4:515–523.

Roberts, A. 1948. "The Editor's Page." *The Frat* 45:4.

Rodda, M. 1970. *The Hearing-Impaired School Leaver.* London: University of London Press.

Romero, E. 1950. "The Open Forum." *Silent Worker* 2:31.

Rutherford, S. 1983. "Funny in Deaf—Not in Hearing." *Journal of American Folklore* 96:310–322.

Ryle, G. 1949. *The Concept of the Mind.* New York: Barnes and Noble.

Sapir, E. 1921. *Language: An Introduction of the Study of Speech.* New York: Harcourt, Brace, and World.

Schildroth, A. 1980. "Public Residential Schools for Deaf Students in the United States, 1970–1978." *American Annals of the Deaf* 125:80–91.

Siple, P. 1982. "Signed Language and Linguistic Theory." In *Exceptional Language and Linguistics,* eds. L. Obler and L. Menn. New York: Academic.

—————, ed. 1978. *Understanding Language through Sign Language Research.* New York: Academic.

Smolen, P. 1982. "Changing Signs." *Silent News* 14:3.

Stokoe, W. C., Jr. 1960. "Sign Language Structure: An Outline of the Visual Communication System of the American Deaf." *Studies in Linguistics* 8.

Stokoe, W. C., Jr., D. Casterline, and C. Croneberg. 1965. *A Dictionary of American Sign Language on Linguistic Principles.* Washington, D.C.: Gallaudet College Press.

Supalla, S. 1986. "Manually Coded English: The Modality Question in Signed Language Development." Paper presented at the Conference on Theoretical Issues in Sign Language Research, Rochester, N.Y.

Supalla, T. 1978. "Morphology of Verbs of Motion and Location in American Sign Language." Paper presented at the Second National Symposium on Sign Language Research and Teaching, San Diego, Calif.

———— 1985. "The Classifier System in American Sign Language." In *Noun Classification and Categorization,* ed. C. Craig. Philadelphia: Benjamins.

Switzer, M. E., and B. R. Williams. 1967. "Life Problems of Deaf People: Prevention and Treatment." *Archives of Environmental Health* 15:249–256.

Tyger, Tyger. 1967. Indianapolis: Captioned Films for the Deaf, Inc. Film.

U.S. National Center for Health Statistics. 1987. *Data from the National Health Survey,* ser. 10, no. 160, tables 62, 78. Washington, D.C.: Government Printing Office.

Valli, C. 1985. "Windy Bright Morning." Washington, D.C.: Gallaudet College. Video.

Veditz, G. 1913. *Preservation of the Sign Language.* Silver Spring, Md.: National Association of the Deaf. Film.

Wikstrom, L. 1987. "Report on Sweden and Sign Language Research." Presentation given at the Second International Workshop for Deaf Researchers, Leksand, Sweden.

Wilbur, R. 1979. *American Sign Language and Sign Systems.* Baltimore: University Park Press.

———— 1986. "The Interaction of Linguistic Theory and Research on Sign Language." In *The Real-World Linguist: Linguistic Applications in the 1980s,* ed. P. Bjarkman and V. Raskin. Norwood, N.J.: Ablex.

———— 1987. *American Sign Language: Linguistic and Applied Dimensions.* San Diego, Calif.: College Hill Press.

Winzer, M. A. 1986. "Deaf-Mutia: Responses to Alienation by the Deaf in the Mid-Nineteenth Century." *American Annals of the Deaf* 131:29–32.

Woodward, J. 1972. "Implications for Sociolinguistics Research Among the Deaf." *Sign Language Studies* 1:1–7.

———— 1976. "Black Southern Signing." *Language in Society* 5:303–311.

———— 1982. *How You Gonna Get to Heaven If You Can't Talk to Jesus? On Depathologizing Deafness.* Silver Spring, Md.: TJ Publishers.

Index

DATE

MY 11 40
OC 22 '91
DE 08 91
NO 16 '92
DE 13 '93
JUL 19 97
MR 05 08
FE 24 D
OC 23 0

Demco, Inc. 38-293